# Empowered To Win, Third Edition Anthology

# EMPOWERED TO WIN

## 3RD ANTHOLOGY EDITION

### Allison G. Daniels

AGD Publishing
Upper Marlboro, Maryland

*Empowered to Win! 3rd Anthology Edition*
AGD Publishing
Copyright © 2022 By Allison Gregory Daniels

All rights reserved. Under International Copyright Law, no part of this book may be reproduced, distributed, or transmitted in any form by any means, graphic, electronic, or mechanical, including photocopy, recording, taping, or by any information storage or retrieval system, without permission in writing from the author except in the case of reprints in the context of the reviews, quotes, or references.

Printed in the United States of America.

Paperback ISBN: 978-1-7372867-9-0

Cover Design & Layout by Tywebbin Creations

Editor: Sheila Hightower

For details, Email: allisongdaniels@verizon.net or visit us at www.agdpublishing.com

Unless otherwise indicated, scripture quotations are from the Holy Bible, the King James Version.

## TABLE OF CONTENTS

| | |
|---|---|
| *Foreword by Dr. Essie M. McKoy* | ix |
| *Introduction* | 1 |
| **CHAPTER 1**<br>*Winning in the Midst of Trials & Tribulations by Dr. Essie M. McKoy* | 1 |
| **CHAPTER 2**<br>*Winning with Gratitude by Sheila Farr* | 15 |
| **CHAPTER 3**<br>*I Think I Can (But Can I Really?) by Dawn Lieck* | 25 |
| **CHAPTER 4**<br>*The Power of Y.O.U. to Get It! by Rosalind H. Agurs* | 33 |
| **CHAPTER 5**<br>*Destined to Win by Evangelist Tamala J. Coleman* | 45 |
| **CHAPTER 6**<br>*Surrender in Peace by Gizelle Taylor-Daniels* | 53 |
| **CHAPTER 7**<br>*Healed and Free by Elder Felicia Edmond* | 67 |

## CHAPTER 8
*Unbecoming to Become* by Reverend Suzette Hampton — 79

## CHAPTER 9
*Winning Begins Within* by Minister Cathy Henderson — 93

## CHAPTER 10
*Learning to Love the Gift— Me!* by Pastor Valerie Howard-Jones — 107

## CHAPTER 11
*Mourning to Morning* by Reverend Shawnta Moody — 123

## CHAPTER 12
*Finding Love Again by Starting Within* by Christal Spence Newkirk — 133

## CHAPTER 13
*Gracefully Broken: Looking Back to Move Forward* by LuDrean Howard-Peterson — 145

## CHAPTER 14
*Thankful, Grateful and Blessed to Lend a Helping Hand* by Maria Thorpe — 161

## CHAPTER 15
*Empowered to Write— NOW!* by Minister Allison Gregory Daniels — 173

*Biblical Sources* — 183

*Are You Ready (Finally) to Write Your Story?* — 185

*Books Published by AGD Publishing* — 187

*Published Books by Visionary Allison G. Daniels* — 189

*Books Authored by Visionary Allison G. Daniels* — 191

*Co-Authored by Allison G. Daniels* — 193

*Book Coach / Consultant* — 195

# FOREWORD

The audacious, international, and award-winning author, Minister Allison G. Daniels, has again, inspired a collective group of women to tell their stories of how they used their trials, tribulations, and challenges in life to make a significant difference as they examined their confidence, faith, and encouragement to win in this journey of life. These stories will motivate, inspire, and encourage readers to reflect on their own life challenges. Readers will be compelled to move forward, knowing that there is a greater authority and, in the process, gain clarity about their purpose and to develop confidence in standing strong during their challenging circumstances and situations and be victorious in how they continue to navigate life.

This book speaks not only to the minds and hearts of readers, but to the core of the souls of readers. It uplifts your spirit and gives hope to the darkest circumstances. It gives joy and a sense of peace to know that they overcame obstacles that seemed insurmountable, and they came out better on the other side! They believed and knew that they were not alone on their journey!

These stories were not only a compilation of challenges that these women encountered, but their faith was tested, their confidence shaken, and their ability to be encouraged was shattered. In James 1:12, it states "Blessed is the man that endureth temptation: for when he is tried, he shall receive the crown of life, which the Lord hath promised to them that love him." We read herein that the man who remains steadfast under trial, for when he has stood the test he will receive the crown of life, which God has promised to those who love Him. God's love can help us reach any mountaintop, walk through any valley, and see the rainbow after a tumultuous storm.

Truly, in life, we do not know our journey or path in advance, and we do not know the race we will have to run, and, also, we do not know what lies ahead. So, these powerful stories will cause you to reexamine the path you have travelled, look at the races you have run, and look ahead with optimism; so, if they did it, you can too! You will gain the ability to be constructive and not destructive in your approach, no matter the circumstances you face.

Each chapter will give you a glimpse into the reality of what the author encountered. These authors share authentically, and you will learn how they took their challenges and turned them into opportunities. You will gain effective strategies and techniques, as well as scriptures that will help you embrace your fears and overcome your battles. It will help you to see that sometimes your story may not be what you perceive. However, if you move forward with the belief that all things are possible, that you will be stronger because of your struggle, and that you will achieve more than what you can conceive, you will be amazed at the outcome of your destiny!

These contributing authors focused on sharing candidly so that they could be a support to readers and provide guidance for future generations. The magnitude of their experiences and their stories are powerful as they pass the baton of knowledge from one generation to the next! They share their greatest success to their deepest sorrow so that you can acquire tips about how to move beyond your lows to reach your highs!

These authors did not look at themselves as great even though they conquered their trials. Their challenges made them better than they were yesterday and prepared them for a future that will provide them the skills needed to assist others on their journey through the issues and problems we encounter in life. Readers will see what these extraordinary women were able to overcome and how they continue to make an impact in the lives of others. These women believed in something greater than their own abilities and their internal convictions.

In this anthology, you will not only gain a better understanding of the stories from each author, but you will hear their pains and sufferings, their heartaches, and how their lives were turned upside down. Some even shared the experience of how they almost gave up on life. The roads that they traveled, the turns they took, and the detours they encountered are compelling.+

Their passion, insight, self-awareness, strength, optimism, hope, and inspiration came out of their challenges and their desire to give back, make a difference, and help the next generation to find the courage to push through even when they wanted to give up. They believed in themselves when no one else did and had the faith that there was a brighter day ahead. Trust and know that the best is yet to come and remember Romans 8:28, "And know that in all things God works for the good of those who love Him, who have been called according to his purpose."

Some of these phenomenal women had to make sacrifices on their journey. They had to forsake their own ambitions and face their internal thoughts of not doing enough, not being enough, and not giving enough to the people they loved to heal and find their own voices, their own space, and their own place in life.

Often, they stretched themselves beyond their own capabilities and recharged to grip with the realities of their situations. As a reader, you will be amazed at the experiences they share and how they became the women they are today.

In times of difficulties, we have self-doubt, we believe we are incapable of winning, and we create stories to sabotage our own dreams. These stories will give you tools that will help you discover your own vulnerabilities and move forward in your quest of what you do not know now that you are capable of on your own journey!

*Empowered to Win* is not just another book! These sheroes share how through unfathomable situations, you can make it to the other side and become the best that you were meant to be. While you read, you will shed a tear and be heart broken, but you will also feel the greatness of their spirits, the tenacity of their will, and the might of their desire to share so that you will be better than you were yesterday and even greater than you will be tomorrow.

As you read and reflect, you will gain a better understanding of your own untapped potential and how these stories can help you bring to life what is inside of you. Learning from these EXTRAORDINARY women and reading their stories will give you the confidence, faith, and encouragement to WIN in life! Philippians 4:13

reminds us that we can do all things through Christ who strengthens us.

Warm Regards,

Dr. Essie M. McKoy
Award-Winning Educator
Six Times Amazon Best Selling Author
Host of #1 Podcast Dr. Essie Speaks Education
President/CEO of Dr. Essie Speaks Educational Consulting, LLC

# INTRODUCTION

### EMPOWERED TO WIN!

Within this *Empowered to WIN* book, each author will walk you through their life experiences and journey of hope and survival in midst of it all. In this book, the authors will share their testimony to the faith that they stood on to bombard Heaven to make a change in their lives, and, also, you will see how they never gave up because they trusted and believed in God. Although they dealt with past disappointments, by God's grace they continued to stay connected to the call and purpose God had for their lives.

### EMPOWERED TO WIN!

In this book *Empowered to WIN*, your journey of wholeness will begin with the power, the praise, and the presence of the Lord. This book will challenge you to take back your life and enable you to walk in your authority so that you can face tomorrow –today.

# WINNING IN THE MIDST OF TRIALS AND TRIBULATIONS

Dr. Essie M. McKoy
Award-Winning Educator
Six Times Amazon Best Selling Author
Host of #1 Podcast Dr. Essie Speaks Education
President/CEO of Dr. Essie Speaks Educational Consulting, LLC

## ABOUT THE AUTHOR

Dr. Essie McKoy received her Doctorate in Education (Ed.D.) and an Educational Specialist Degree (Ed. S.) in Educational Leadership from the University of North Carolina at Greensboro, a master's degree in Middle Grades Education from Appalachian State University, and a Bachelor of Science Degree in Special Education with a certification in Learning Disabilities from Winston-Salem State University. She has additional areas of certification in Public School Administration/Principalship, Curriculum and Instruction with a concentration in English, and the Superintendency. Her dissertation topic, "A Study of Elementary Principals' Perceptions of Accountability and Leadership in an Era of High Stakes Testing," is a foundational part of her book, "The Heart of School Transformation: My Journey into Transforming Urban Schools." She attended The Urban Superintendent's Program at Howard University and The American Association of School Administrators and received the National Superintendent's Certification.

In addition, she attended Harvard University's Public Education Leadership Project Program and many other leadership programs throughout the nation, including the Wake Forest University Leadership Program for

Public Engagement, The Distinguished Leadership Program and the Distinguished Leadership Digital Learning Program at North Carolina State University, The Principals' Executive Program – Leadership Program for Assistant Principals at the University of North Carolina at Chapel Hill and received the Program's Outstanding Academic Achievement Award and she graduated from the Principals' Executive Program – Leadership Program for New Principals at the University of North Carolina at Chapel Hill where she received the prestigious Jack McCall Award. Dr. McKoy also attended the Mastering Leadership Dynamics Program with the BB&T Institute, as well as three other programs at BB&T. In addition, she was accepted into The National Scholars Honor Society. A highlight of her career is that she was selected by Winston Salem State University as the Education Alumni Achiever Recipient.

Dr. McKoy began her teaching career at an alternative middle school and later taught a "regular" middle school. She has served as assistant principal at the elementary level before becoming the principal of two elementary schools. She worked as an instructor at the Math and Science Academy of Excellence at Winston-Salem State University and worked as an Adjunct Professor at NC A&T State University and ITT Technical Institute and served as a Hybrid Instructor at George Mason University. Furthermore, she served as an Executive

Director/Principal at the middle school level and has experience at the high school level in the area of special education as a Department Chair. Her experience spans from pre-K through college and she uses her experience and knowledge to continue to make an impact in the field of education. Dr. McKoy was nominated for the AASA Women in School Leadership Award with the Bill and Melinda Gates Foundation. In addition, she received the Educator of the Year Award and The Executive Citation of Anne Arundel County Maryland Award. Dr. McKoy has been featured in K.I.S.H., BSM, SwagHer, Glambitious, PowerHouse Global, She Speaks, Creating Your Seat at the Table, and UP WORDS (Edutopia) magazines. She has received many accolades and recognitions for her accomplishments throughout her extensive career.

She is known as a transformational leader and has improved the academic performance and success indicators of all the schools she has led. She is proud of the fact that both elementary schools became Piedmont Triad Signature Schools- the highest growth schools. Her mission is to continue to ignite a passion for others and to make a profound impact in the field of education.

She is the President and CEO of her own Educational Consulting Business, Dr. Essie Speaks. She travels the nation to do speaking engagements and is an Amazon Six-

Time Best-selling author. Dr. McKoy has written extensively and continues to contribute to a wide variety of nationwide writing projects. She has written as an author, contributing author, and a foreword author. Her books are: The Heart of School Transformation; My Journey into Transforming Urban Schools, Coaching Champions- How to understand the players before giving the plays; A Guide to Improvement and Success, Women of Virtue: Walking in Excellence, Leadership Tidbits, and The Grylfriend Code Sorority Edition, Vision and Purpose; Inspiring Our Community, and Women Who Lead; Extraordinary Women with Extraordinary Achievements – Featuring School Principals.

In addition, she continues to work in her area of expertise for a local school district in the DMV and writes for Vision and Purpose Lifestyle Magazine. Furthermore, you will hear Dr. McKoy every Sunday at 5:30 PM EST, hosting her #1 Podcast Show, Dr. Essie Speaks Education! She is a member of Alpha Kappa Alpha Sorority Incorporated! She invites you to visit her web site at www.dressiespeaks.com and keep abreast of updates on all social media platforms.

# CHAPTER 1
## *Winning in the Midst of Trials and Tribulations*

Trials and tribulations will come, no matter your relationship with God, how well you live, what kind of house you live in, what kind of car you drive, your financial or educational status, the accomplishments or accolades you have received, the connections you have, what brand name clothes you wear, the diamonds, pearls, or furs you own or what worldly possessions you hold dear. Trials and tribulations will come when you least expect them and how you least expect them! In James 1:2, we are reminded to, "Count it all joy, my brothers, when you meet trials of various kinds." (ESV)

Life can throw curveballs and make us walk in the lowest valley and never gaze at the mountaintop. It can cause us to drown in our own story in which we create in our own minds. It can cause us to never look at the stars and dare to see the north star. It can cause us to look in the forest and never see the trees. It can cause us to second guess who we are, whose we are, and what plan God has designed for our lives.

There are times that we get tired of dealing with the same heartaches and headaches. We get tired of the mess ups and mistakes we face. We get tired of asking questions and never finding the right answers. We get tired of opening the next chapter and never getting to the end. We get tired of facing our demons and staring at our struggles. We get tired of the desire to move forward, but always finding ourselves going backwards. We get tired of standing tall in the crowd when we cannot stand tall in private. We get tired of every no to what we believe should be yes. We get tired of searching for love and feeling the hollow heart. We get tired of the setbacks to our dreams. We get tired of restarting with the same goals and never making progress. We get tired of the rainy days and dark nights. We get tired of lack of peace and the internal turmoil. We get tired of the unrest we encounter in our world. We get tired of putting the public mask on when we wrestle with the private mask. We get tired of trying to find our calling and not yielding to who and what God wants us to be. We get tired of listening to the same story and hearing the same ending. We get tired of the same song with the same lyrics. We get tired of the mundane life and the stress we face. We get tired of the skeletons in our closet and the lies we tell. We get tired of the posturing to move to the next phase. In the end, we realize we get tired of just being tired!

On our journey we will run into roadblocks, detours, unforeseen circumstances, and untraveled paths. We might even find ourselves in a place where we become weary and want to give up on life. We halt our ability to navigate to the next place and space in our lives.

Yes, these life challenges hurt, they make use cry, they make us question is there a God, they halt our progression, they hinder our faith, they give volume to our fears, they keep us in a holding pattern, and they make us want to throw in the towel. We become bitter, depressed, sad, angry, upset, feel worthless and hopeless, and ultimately it brings out the worst in us. We isolate ourselves and we depart from our relationships, we keep people at bay, we disengage with life and the world, we try to change our identity, and last but not least, we sometimes sabotage our own destiny.

During times of difficulties, we often reflect on the experiences and ask ourselves who do we turn to? What are we going to do now that we are faced with these challenges? When do we decide to move forward, or will we just give up? Where will we go to seek help to be restored, or do we just remain neutral amid the difficulties? How will we navigate these challenging times? All this is part of the process of encountering and trying to deal with our reality. Times like this will cause us to question our own faith, belief, and strength in God!

It is amazing how we can believe more money in our bank account will eliminate all our trials and tribulations. We tend to think the bigger our investments, the less we will have to deal with life's problems. We think that the more friends we have in our inner circle will cause our challenges to dissipate. We think that the bigger our house, the more we will find comfort in living in luxury. We think that the more exotic car we drive will allow us to ride away our trials and tribulations. We believe that the farthest we travel we will escape the challenges we face. We even think that our skills, abilities, and special talents will give us privilege to a life without difficulties. We think that a high paying position will be enough to pay for the trials we deal with day-to-day. Sometimes, we even think that bringing life into this world will cause us to find solace and exempt us from tribulations. After we have achieved all that we can and done all that we can, if we are still in a place wrestling with our inner spirit, allowing fear to overshadow our ability to live in our purpose, not mastering our trials and tribulations, and not allowing God to be the source of our wins and successes, we are underserving our soul and underperforming based on what God has designed us to be in this life.

Without a shadow of doubt and with strong faith, I declare that there is a God who can help you overcome every fear you have ever encountered. He will give you the ability to walk with giants and leap over every obstacle you perceive as challenges. Those challenges will become your greatest opportunities. He can help you overcome every setback and make it your setup. He can cause your sleepless nights to become your place of dreams and visions for a brighter future. He can give you the fortitude and the latitude to maneuver through any difficult situation. He can give you the ability to hope when you see no hope. He can create the right circumstances during your most difficult times. He can give you what you need when you need it and fill your emptiness with peace and love. In Romans 8:28, "And we know that for those who love God all things work together for good for those who are called according to his purpose." (ESV) Trust God! Give your worries to Him; have faith that He can do all things; be patient in tribulation, be constant in prayer and understanding during your times of difficulties; and believe in His power to calm your storms.

No matter what you go through and when you go through, do not give up and do not give in! Keep moving forward, step-by-step, day-by-day, and most importantly, revisit your relationship with God. Reconnect to the source of life, reconnect to the core of your existence, and reconnect to your divine purpose. Sometimes in life, we encounter trials and tribulations because it was all a part of the Master's plan. Not to say that God is the maker of these tumultuous experiences, but sometimes we go through, to become stronger, more productive, and a better version of ourselves. It gives us the opportunity to be more appreciative, to share our journey with others, to give back in a way that we never imagined, to seek God even more, and to live a life designed the way God wants it to be! Allow each trial and tribulation to teach you something. Learn the lesson from what you have gone through and that will give you the strength to grow and become stronger!

Sit and listen to your own thoughts but take time to listen to God. He talks to us constantly; lean on Him during times of hurt, pain, sorrow, and challenges. All we need do is be quiet, be still, and adhere to the thoughts He gives us. In Psalms 46:10, we must be reminded to, "Be still and know that I am God; I will be exalted among the nations, I will be exalted in the earth." (ESV)

Every day of our lives, we can meditate and pray for God to give us the strength to navigate life's most difficult times. We can rely on Him to give us the courage to deal with our woes. We must remember that God is always there, all we need do is call on Him! Ask God to strengthen your faith in Him and allow your faith to guide you through. Read and encourage your spirit. When you are down and out about a particular issue, do not dwell on the issue, but read the Word of God and find out how God can allow you to see things differently, gain a new and different perspective.

At times, we may need to seek advice from professionals who can help us work through our difficulties. It is always an effective strategy when we can talk about our trials and tribulations to another person, and they can listen intensely. They can listen and they can ask all the right questions to get to the root cause of the issue, and they help us to reach a conclusion that will allow us to move forward in a positive and productive way. There are times when we must prioritize our lives and think strategically about how we will go through the trials we encounter. We put what is important to us first and proceed to rank according to the next priority, until we have exhausted the list of options as to how we will address going through our temporary storm. While we turn to others in times of need, be careful or be mindful if their advice will work for you and your situation. Remember to always trust your instincts and follow your heart.

After you have cleared your mind, reached the depths of your soul, sought God to help you navigate your trials, and you have succeeded, despite your tribulations, and learned some valuable lessons along the way, remember to offer a word of advice and encouragement to help others to overcome. Engage in a conversation that will give help to others so that they can see things objectively; encourage others to keep looking ahead and remind them that this too shall pass. Our stories were meant to be told and not for us to hold! We must grow in our faith, confidence, and ability to reach our full potential. Overcoming our trials and tribulations is a process that allows us to grow stronger, wiser, and deeper in navigating to find the true essence of our existence, our purpose, and the vision set for our lives.

## REFLECTION QUESTIONS:

1. What trials and tribulations are you facing?
2. Think about the who, what, when, where, and how of your trials and tribulations as I referred to in this chapter and record your responses to each.
3. What strategies will you employ to address your trials and tribulations?
4. What scriptures can you refer to that will help you go through and get through this phase?

# WINNING WITH GRATITUDE

Sheila Farr
CEO of Gulf Coast Training &
Education Services, LLC
Founder of Biloxi Reads! Program

## ABOUT THE AUTHOR

Sheila Farr is an eternal optimist! After 20 years of building and managing successful businesses for others, she stepped out and started her own business in 2017. Ms. Farr is now the CEO of Gulf Coast Training & Education Services, LLC, in Biloxi, Mississippi, where she helps individuals and small businesses overcome obstacles and achieve their dreams by developing personalized business strategies that work.

She is ABD (All But Dissertation) for her doctorate in Organizational Leadership; holds masters' degrees in Health & Wellness Counseling and in Adult Education, is a RYT-200 yoga instructor, a SHRM-SCP certified Human Resources Director, and a Lean/Six Sigma blackbelt. Sheila has been teaching yoga for over 11 years and is a Certified Yoga Continuing Education provider through the Yoga Alliance.

Sheila is a 13-times best-selling author and a cheerleader for others. She motivates people through her blog, "Thankful and Blessed 365," and is the founder of "Biloxi Reads!," a literacy initiative along the Mississippi Gulf Coast. Sheila also enjoys serving her community and the state of Mississippi as the Workforce Readiness Director for both the regional and state chapters of the Society for Human Resource Management.

Sheila loves to connect with people via her website: www.gulfcoasttraining.org or on social media sites such as Facebook, Instagram and LinkedIn.

Facebook: https://www.facebook.com/trainthegulfcoast

IG: https://www.instagram.com/shefarr37/

LinkedIn: https://www.linkedin.com/in/sheila-farr-20b35142/

Blog site: https://thankfulandblessed365.com/

# Chapter 2
# Winning with Gratitude

*"A stumbling block to the pessimist is a stepping-stone to the optimist."* — *Eleanor Roosevelt*

Oftentimes we fail to see possibilities because we are so conditioned to only see the obstacles in our lives. I was guilty of this in my business life several years ago, but then something changed that opened my heart and my mind to a world of winning that I could never imagine; that "thing" was gratitude!

I will never forget the word that changed my professional life forever: acquisition. For nearly six years, I had worked days, nights, weekends, and holidays to build a dynamic team of high-producing professionals who loved their work and achieved unbelievable results in patient care and business. In essence we had a well-balanced team, who loved what they did and worked hard to stay at the top of their game. That's why, on the day I heard the "a" word – my whole heart sank, and I hung my head in total defeat.

You see, when you're working to build someone else's dream, you put the key to your happiness in someone else's pocket. You give them complete control of your livelihood and your ability to impact others, and the work they do. When you work for other people, it's true that you don't have the responsibility, liability, and risk that they cover, but you also do not have the ability to make decisions that impact your own life...or the lives of others.

As the Lord would have it, just prior to the time that my professional world fell apart, my personal life fell into place. Having just gone through a divorce — and feeling very alone and confused – my mind was in a condition of what I like to call "stinking thinking". That means that I really wasn't trusting God in the way I should've been trusting Him; so many of my thoughts were negative, and I was filled with frustration, confusion, doubt, and fear. I was focusing on all the things that were going wrong in my life instead of focusing on everything that was going right! Truly, this is one of the amazing things that I love about the Lord: When He breaks you down to the point of nothing, He's getting you ready to be built up to greatness. That's exactly what happened to me! I started making it a habit to daily write down the things for which I was thankful. Then, I took those things and made them public, so that people would hold me accountable in continuing to do this. In just a few weeks, the Lord had transformed my mind, and the changes that would soon follow in my life, were unbelievably good. He changed me from the inside out, allowing me to see that my stumbling blocks were really the stepping-stones to what could help me navigate my way from building something for other people to building something new for myself.

Prior to the acquisition (the acquirements) at my workplace, my friends and other small business owners would often come to me for help in starting their businesses or looking at processes and strategies for reinventing their struggling businesses. After doing this for a few years as a "side hustle" for a few friends, those closest to me urged me to open my own business and start working to grow my own training company. That was a huge dream for me, and at the time, I wasn't used to dreaming that big for myself. I couldn't dream like that for myself because I was sowing into someone else's dream and putting all my efforts, all my talent, and all my hard work into building someone else's business. However, when the Lord changed my perspective on life, He also planted a new heart of confidence within me, which was something new to me, so I quickly learned to embrace it.

In 2017, I started my little training company. I say "little training company" because at first, I just taught a few yoga classes and a couple of entry-level medical billing classes. As word got out to the masses about what I was doing, I began to receive more and more calls; consequently, my company continued to grow and thrive even the more, even though I was only putting my part-time effort into it.

I was a fearless leader when it came to running someone else's company, but running my own business was very new to me. Initially, I wanted to withdraw and return to my "lack of" mentality, but the Lord had other plans for me. I was no longer operating within a spirit of brokenness; the Lord catapulted me deeper into my own business and started opening doors, windows, and even breaking down barriers to get me to new places and in front of new people. I often say I received a "Holy push" to start sowing into my own business. By sowing into my own business, I would be able to make a positive impact once again on the personal growth and development of others. I could once again provide relevant work training and business strategy sessions to people who needed them. Once I surrendered to God's will and call on my life to serve others in small businesses, my confidence increased, my small business grew, and my passion and joy for my work was restored!

So, if you're struggling right now because you feel unsettled in the job you're currently in, maybe it's time for you to make a change… or maybe it's time for you to do a little "inside work" on yourself that will allow you to get closer to the Lord and become more aligned with the plans and purpose He has in store for you. If you really want to thrive in times of adversity, one of the best ways I've found to do that is simply to be true to yourself. When you're walking and working in your purpose according to the gifts that the Lord has given you – and in the way that He has called you to do it – you cannot fail. When an acquisition rocked my world and sent me into an ocean of uncertainty in my life, I was forced to reevaluate the way I'd been living and the work I was doing. The Lord opened doors for me, and I simply obeyed and walked through them. I was also planning and preparing as I went along, so I would be ready to transition when the time was right. In all honesty, though, I was scared, I thought a corporate 9-5 job provided me stability and consistency, but while in the middle of an acquisition, I found out that when you work for someone else, you have absolutely no control over what happens to you; and things can change at any time. That realization forced me to trust God more deeply and prepare myself more completely.

To help you win – whether it be in business or life – let me encourage you to honestly answer a few questions. The answers to these questions will begin to help you see where you can make some positive changes in your own life so that you can either: a) start winning, or b) continue winning! The key to winning – no matter what you're working toward – is keeping the Lord in the center of your life and constantly seeking Him in all you do! He has proven to me over and over that I could win at all things, just so long as I keep my eye on Him...and continuously keep gratitude in my heart.

## Questions to Ponder:

1. What three things in your life are you most grateful for?
2. What are the top five gifts God has blessed you with?
3. Describe what living a successful life looks like to you.

# I THINK I CAN! (BUT CAN I REALLY?)

Dawn Lieck
CEO, Finally Free, LLC,
Dawn Lieck Enterprise

## ABOUT THE AUTHOR

Dawn Lieck is a world-class business professional with remarkable expertise in the areas of wellness and multidimensional coaching.

A mirrored portrait of what it means to be a "Renaissance Woman", Dawn's abilities have earned her professional respect amongst generational influencers.

Setting the standard in her field, Dawn is an International Speaker, best-selling author, and the CEO of both Finally Free, LLC, and Dawn Lieck Enterprise. Affectionately known as the "Transformation Life Coach", Dawn helps successful professionals harness their true potential by putting them in touch with themselves on an intrinsic level. Having an unyielding passion for personal development, Dawn motivates clients to renew their perspective, conquer their fears, and to create a life balance, using a system of pragmatic strategies.

Dawn's mantra is simple; "DO IT SCARED!".

The results have been phenomenal, as Dawn has enjoyed a wide range of successes and she is also in high demand, from both domestic and international audiences. Dawn has held a three-year consecutive election as one of the Top 100 Women to Know, on the Gulf Coast, where she was also featured as a Woman of Achievement Entrepreneur Finalist.

Though her talents lead her reputation, her heart for service leads her path, as Dawn is involved in many organizations on the Gulf Coast, including the Gulfport Chamber of Commerce Board, Back Bay Mission Advisory Council, Leadership Gulf Coast Graduate, VP Membership Chair for Lighthouse Business and Professional Women, Chair for Success Women's Conference and a team lead for women at Habitat for Humanity.

Email: Dawn@dawnlieckenterprise.com

Facebook: Dawn Lieck

# Chapter 3
# I Think I Can! (But Can I Really?)

Oh, my goodness! The conversations we have with ourselves! Sometimes they aren't all friendly or positive; I'm sure we all can agree!

For as long as I can remember, I always felt as if I was meant for so much more than where I was initially. Whether it was my job or my personal relationships, I felt as if there was so much more for me. You will notice that I used the word "felt" vs. how I acted.

That little, small voice was steadily chatting in the back of my head, saying things like; "You can do it Girl!" Then in the next breath she would say, "Well maybe you could if you knew how." or she would say "You could if you were good enough to pull it off." "You really could, if you had enough experience like the other entrepreneurs, you see doing things." I tell you that her chatting was absolute and endless. Whenever I felt strong and confident of a newly devised plan, she would commence with her negativity until I placed my plan back in the tiny box where it seemed to stay most of the time. I mean after all she had some valid points. You see that voice was constantly telling me and reminding me of the many reasons why I couldn't accomplish my goals, and I couldn't beat her numbers with reasons why I could.

## I THINK I CAN! (BUT CAN I REALLY?)

This is such a hard battle to win with ourselves. Brutal, actually! Many of you might agree that it's so much easier to concede than it is to fight to win! This battle raged within me for years. Miss Negative Nancy (I call her) and her steady voice of mediocre expectations of me seemed to be my fate.

As a result, here is what I learned to be true: That her negative voice would unquestionably be the truth of my destiny, as long as I believed and accepted what she was telling me. Our minds are so powerful in every aspect of our lives. I had experienced missed (lost or ruined) opportunities by over thinking and listening to that endless chatter in my head.

I am a firm believer that God will take you exactly where He wants you to go and in His timing, when He wants you to get there. I had been listening to that negative voice telling me that I could not succeed for far too long; telling me that I was not worthy and that everyone else was better than me for so long, that I held it as my truth. So much so that I had deafened myself to hearing what God had been telling me all along, that I was worthy and that I was meant for so much more, and that I had a purpose.

As soon as I opened my heart, my eyes and my ears, my path was laid out for me and my success in business, as well as my personal life, began to flourish in miraculous ways!

When I look back at myself, concerning my faith walk, I felt as if I had faith in God at the time, however, in actuality, I had faltered in my faith. I had chosen to listen to my own negativity and fear instead of having faith in my Creator and knowing that He had a purpose for me. It's not like I didn't know I was destined for more from the beginning, but the fact is that I chose to believe otherwise. In doing so, I lived a life that was nowhere near happy or prosperous. There was always an emptiness within me. That emptiness was my lack of faith and my disobedience.

I've since learned to listen, pray on things, wait for my answer from God, and when it's given, I will not allow fear to stop or grip me from being obedient in the assignment. Having faith, conquering fear, and being obedient is not always a flawless process on my part. The chatter still surfaces from time to time however, the difference is that now I know how to quiet the negative chatter before it consumes my actions. I quiet Negative Nancy through prayer. I know now that all things are possible through Christ, and I am open to listen for His leading and direction.

My business is growing in leaps and bounds. God has truly given me the man of my dreams 56 years into my life, to grow old with. Everything I felt I could do I'm now doing through faith in God and my belief in myself. I have a completely different life now. I have not only the love of my life, but the love I was destined to have from the beginning.

I will leave you with some thoughts to ponder. These three questions are a self-check and will give you the answer as to whether you are listening and if you really are, to whom?

## TAKE A MINUTE

1. What are the goals and dreams of your heart? (They were placed there.)
2. What's your plan of obedience to accomplish these things?
3. Are you walking in faith or listening to self chatter?

Your choices will always be yours. Mediocre? Ordinary? It's time to decide!

# THE POWER OF Y.O.U. TO GET TO IT!

Rosalind H. Agurs
"Radiant Roz"
Author, Creator, Administrative Consultant
Website: www.RadiantRoz.com

## ABOUT THE AUTHOR

Rosalind (Roz) Agurs serves in the capacities of author, consultant, real estate broker and entrepreneur. With an innate ability to advise and teach, Roz loves to harness the power of the moment to disciple others in the richness of Christian living and in the joy of the gift of life!

A published author, Roz is committed to producing action-taking resources that result in victorious living! Her literary work, "FEAR NOT! A 52 Week Action Devotional," is an impactful seller. In her vocational assignment as an Executive Administrator, Rosalind shines in creating effective, efficient systems and processes for organizational growth, office management, event facilitation, and spiritual development. She will launch a consulting services firm in 2022 and is the developer of two action forward models, WOOT and Action Required! Rosalind and her husband, Ben, own Success Realty & Property Management, a brokerage firm that assists and educates clients in the home buying/selling process. Rosalind seeks to radiate the earth with the light of God, and she lives by the intrinsic values of faith, family, integrity, courage, and commitment.

## CHAPTER 4
## THE POWER OF Y.O.U. TO GET TO IT!

Reader, Reader!! What a treasure trove of gems you have in your hands as you read through this collection of stories that can and will enhance your "win" game and confirm that you have within YOU what it takes to win again and again!!

You are now gassed (empowered) and ready—-but what will you do? Will you get to it or wait for it to happen? O, my sister, or brother, I have been here time and time again...empowered, yet sitting; empowered but waiting for it to just happen; empowered but procrastinating one more week; empowered yet embittered by all I've had to endure, empowered but allowing my fears to grip and paralyze my movement, so you get the picture, right? I have had to really OWN the fact that I am the one with the power to get to it! I am the only one who can really make the changes, the shift, if you will, that will move me to the win!! And so, it is with you, my friend. By owning the power of YOU to say yes to the assignment and yielding yourself to get to it, you move to the win! By considering the options of getting to it OR waiting for it, and then optimizing the opportunity, you move to the win! And lastly, by realizing and reminding yourself of the uniqueness YOU bring to the assignment, opportunity or occasion and having the unmitigated gall to get to it, you move to the win!!

Allow me to be transparent, I still must tap into the power of ME as I evolve into all I'm created to be as well as all I desire to accomplish during our short life span on earth. I endeavor to impact and influence innumerable individuals to daily be a divine display of living well and living right! Travel with me as I share with you some of my journeys, and candidly implore YOU to own the power within you and go beyond being empowered to win and GET TO IT!

Take the publishing of my first book, FEAR NOT! A 52 Week Action Devotional, I knew that producing this resource was my next project. The book idea was placed on my heart about ten years ago (yes, I said ten!), and it had been reiterated by many confirmations, signs, sayings, sermons, situations, and sisterly nudges along the way…EMPOWERED, RIGHT? I was growing in the study of the Bible and empowered myself by repeating, declaring, affirming over and over, and memorizing countless Scripture verses until they became a natural part of my "reactions" and response when the daily of life was presented (i.e., worry, decisions, bills, tests, trials, etc.). EMPOWERED, RIGHT? Even further, there was the knowing that I had been instructed by God to write, and as Believers, we know we are to obey and trust God, right? So, I had the "empowerment," (the gas, the juice, the pump ups, the instruction, the vision), I then needed to own the power of ME and get to it!! And guess what? I finally DID!! I took ownership of the power of me to GET TO IT! How? First, I said yes to the assignment, and I then yielded myself to the time, energy, focus and nuances of getting the book done. Second, I researched the options to bringing the book to fruition and I reminded myself of the privileged opportunity God would afford me to encourage people to cultivate the Word of God in their hearts and develop the 'fear not' stance or attitude. Third, I recounted how God has uniquely designed and intentionally purposed me, and I unapologetically chose to believe that I, (yes, me with all my flaws, idiosyncrasies, and hesitancy) could champion this endeavor. What happened? Well, because I got to it and got it done, the book has been published, broadly purchased, and presented in several media interviews! But what thrills me the most, is that through my obedience and getting to it, countless lives have been impacted to win over the "reaction" of fear and develop the FEAR NOT stance! Wow!!! Owning the power of YOU to move forward to getting "it" done will land you in the winning zone, too!

### *APPLICATION:* **PAUSE AND THINK:**

What is that specific something you have been "told" to do or led to do and you have not gotten to it yet?" Write down your response as a reminder and a call to action to own the power of You.

I hear oftentimes that "somebody, somewhere, is waiting on you." Your unique make up, your gifts, your talents, and your innate desire to do that special thing must not be placed on the top shelf and laid aside. You, yes, YOU, have the power to get to it! Whatever it is...raising your children in the admonition of the Lord AND educating them on personal and generational wealth; building a tiny house community; getting a patent for that idea you think won't go against the similar idea already out there; teaching a course online, losing weight or deciding to pursue whole life healthiness; starting a non-profit to help a specific segment of the population; or even up leveling your home environment to coincide with the now season of your life — whatever it is, YOU have the power, ability, and strength to accomplish the task. You just need to own the power of YOU and get to it!!

### *Ponder This Scenario:*

Think of getting in your car to go to a specific destination. The car is full of gas, ready to go. However, you sit there with the destination in mind; you continue to sit there, and, in your mind, you see the roads you will take to get you there. You see the building, the lights, the scenery, the occasion, the people you will encounter, the impact and influence you'll have by interacting and sharing; however, you still sit there in the car, no movement. Time passes, nothing happens.

You. Are. Going. Absolutely. Nowhere. But the car is "empowered" right? After all, sufficient gas is in the tank and the key is ready to be turned. Yet it takes the power of YOU to get to the win by use of the car that you empowered to go! How do you own the power of YOU in this scenario? I'm glad you asked! You get in the car; you buckle up your seatbelt and you say Yes! By saying this, you are yielding to the ways and means to get to your destination. When you crank the engine, you are optimizing the option (via a choice) and the opportunity to get there! Pushing the pedal or 'hitting the gas' engages your unique ability to maneuver the vehicle and you are on your way. You have owned the power of YOU to get to it!!! Now by your driving and directing the "empowered" vehicle to the destination, you move to see the "win" come to pass!!

I implore you, GET TO IT!! You have been empowered with the necessary ability, skills, and panache to take the assignment by the horns and win.

But what if it's healing or winning over sickness or a

diagnosis? Owning the power of YOU to get to it still works!! I've been there. My daughter was diagnosed with a chronic kidney dis-ease when she was five years old. Imagine the emotions, fear, and thoughts surrounding this issue. As parents and having a belief and faith in God, we were spiritually empowered to overcome this situation. Thus, we prayed and inquired of the Lord; we outlined and listened to healing scriptures to meditate upon, and we continually and consistently played uplifting worship music in the background of our daughter's room at all times. We also empowered ourselves with the practical: we prayed about it, we acquired kidney information, doing the necessary research, and exploring all the options to make a quality decision. So, yes, we were empowered, but what next? My husband owned the power of YOU and said yes to giving our daughter one of his kidneys. He yielded to the mandate, he optimized the opportunity, and he used his uniqueness (he was a perfect match!) to GET TO IT and provide a win-win for the situation at hand. By God's grace, they are both in great health today and will continue to live long and strong! We won and we win!! And so can YOU! Own your empowerment and show up ready to do the work to get you to there, to get you to the win, and be committed to it for as long as it takes! YOU have everything you need on the inside of you, and YOU can deploy YOU to tackle the assignment and win over every obstacle or challenge.

Allow me to say that even after you've secured a win, pushback and challenges may try to hop up or reappear. My daughter had to have a 2nd kidney transplant at sixteen years of age. This time she had to submit to dialysis treatment for eight months and she had to be placed on a list to receive a kidney. Wow... another parental moment of trepidation; more alarm, more pressing thoughts trying to weigh us down. However, we knew what to do. We called on our faith empowerment, accepted the assignment to be a divine display of God's healing power, and submitted to the process with the win in sight. The joyful result was she received a kidney in record time and by a unique surgeon on duty! We owned the power of YOU, by saying yes and yielding, by optimizing the options available and by using our uniqueness to be an example to others to exhibit joy while going through a difficult time. In other words, we GOT TO IT, in agreement with our daughter, and as a team, we won!!!

## *APPLICATION:* **PAUSE AND THINK**:

Close your eyes. Take a deep breath. See yourself at the finish line of your assignment, your goal, your challenge. What did you accomplish?

How does it feel? Write a note to yourself, celebrating the successful win that YOU said yes to; that YOU yielded to, and that YOU optimized, utilizing your uniqueness to get to the win.

_____

_____

_____

_____

Oh, dear reader, my prayer is that this chapter has stirred your faith, removed all doubts and shaken the complacency, as well as the removal of any negative thoughts, so that you will arise and conquer every assignment, every task, and the God-directed desires of your heart, at every stage of life. It comes down to this –and you've heard it before...YOU must remember, it's the doing that strengthens us. Yes, you are empowered; Yes, you have the information, the necessary skills, the money and the resources, the contacts, etc. Yes, to all the above. But will those things, alone, get you to the win? YOU will have to engage and GET TO IT!! A famous Bible teacher often quotes, "You can sit in a garage all day long, but that doesn't make you a car!" I love that quote because it rings true that a place doesn't define who you are. I boldly say, 'You can be empowered to win; however, YOU can't sit gassed up, ready-to-go all day and think you will just get to your destination!' What if I had gathered all the information for my book and left it typed in the computer? What if you studied for your driver's license and never went for the test? What if I allow the flare-ups of rheumatoid arthritis to stop me from writing, walking, encouraging others and maximizing my life? What if you dressed out in workout clothes to exercise, turned on the exercise video and then just watched it -to only do the moves in your head? (LOL, I've done this, trust me...you won't get to the win!) What if you keep saying "what if"? I'll ask you again: Do you get the picture? It's time to own the power of Y.O.U. and GET TO IT! YOU must say Yes, and yield to the empowerment within you! You must consider the options and optimize the opportunity at hand. YOU must realize and unleash your potential and your uniqueness, which is how you are wired, what you bring to the table, your flair, your God-given talents and giftings, and any other unique abilities you have within you. When you know that you are empowered to win and you own the power of Y.O.U. to GET TO IT, you will find yourself propelling forward to face assignments, ideas, tasks, and all that comes along in the process of the journey! And you will experience successful win after win after win. I'm rooting for you and calling the power of Y.O.U. to arise and come through!

# DESTINED TO WIN

Evangelist Tamala J. Coleman
Bestselling Author, Director, Producer
Owner of NSpire Christian Magazine

## ABOUT THE AUTHOR

Tamala Jenise Coleman is a 2x Bestselling Author, and the author of a total of 9 books; she is also a Director and Producer of Stage Plays and Films.

Tamala is the Founder and Editor and Chief of NSpire Christian Magazine. Tamala strives to empower women and inspire the masses with the power of faith. She is a warrior by heart who has risen above adversities. She has always had an incredible passion for writing which inspired her to pen down her adversities, experiences, and triumphs to empower women and foster the roots of self-belief and self-confidence.

Tamala is also a member of "Women's with Wings" Foundation and she is on the Board of Directors. This foundation is Christian based and it assists women who have been entrapped in Domestic Violence and Sex Trafficking. Tamala also hosts a Radio Show on TalkZone Radio, where she interviews ministers, authors, business owners and people who have a testimony to share with the world, as well as sharing the Good News of Jesus Christ.

# Chapter 5
# Destined to Win

*"Who is it that overcomes the world? Only the one who believes that Jesus is the Son of God." 1 John 5:5 (NIV)*

Did you know you are Destined to Win? As a child of the Most-High God, you are filled with His conquering power. You are filled with the power to overcome all the negative, self-defeating forces of the world. Do you know what that power is? It's your faith. When you activate your faith, you are tapping into His unlimited strength and His Unlimited Power. You are opening the door for Him to move supernaturally in your life.

What is faith: It indicates a belief or conviction with the complementary idea of trust. Faith is not a mere intellectual stance, but a belief that leads to action. So, we understand that faith causes you to live your life differently. It causes you to speak and act differently than you did before. "For faith is the substance of things hoped for and evidence of things not seen.

When things come against you, instead of complaining and giving up, faith causes you to rise-up and say no weapon formed against me shall prosper. I am well able to do ALL things through Christ who gives me strength.

Faith causes you to obey God's Word and do the right thing, even when the wrong thing is happening.

When you choose to live the life of faith, you are choosing God's best. You are choosing a blessing. You are choosing to allow His conquering power to flow through and in you and in every area of your life!

In my life I have leaned on my faith more, especially when things are complicated and when life seems to be somewhat hectic and difficult. Faith and my trust in God have been my leaning posts because I realized I am nothing without God.

Herein, lately, I have learned about overcoming in my life, even in my 53 years of living. In fact, I have found that the Lord gave me what I needed to overcome in a season of discouragement –in a season of despair. He will always show us who we are in Christ.

What do you wish you could overcome? Maybe it's harmful patterns of thinking; maybe it's a destructive habit; maybe it's emotional struggles of fear, anxiety, discouragement, anger, or bitterness. The Lord desires for us to be OVERCOMERS!

It would be nice if you could speak a quick prayer and the Lord would wave His magic wand and you would immediately be free from your troubles. But as you examine Scriptures carefully, you realize that the Lord allows us to go through trials and tribulations so that He can show Himself in our lives that through Christ we are Overcomers.

I am a living witness that God will use your pain for your purpose, and that purpose He has for you was already ordained before the foundation of the world. In my life I had to learn to see myself as God sees me: as a woman of God who is fearfully and wonderfully made. I make it a daily affirmation to speak a faith-filled word over my life.

One of my favorite Scriptures is found in Jeremiah 29:11 – "For I know the thoughts that I think toward you, saith the Lord, thoughts of peace, and not of evil, to give you an expected end." (KJV)

Please understand that God couldn't think of you without having plans for you. He's too complete to leave things undone, halfway finished and incomplete. What you see as unfinished God has already seen it finished. What you see as impossible or a dead-end, God sees it as complete and done.

The same is true for YOUR salvation. When relatives saw you as a heathen, God saw you as holy! When friends saw you as defeated, God saw you as divine! Even when the "church" folk saw you as a hopeless case, God saw you as His Child! You are an OVERCOMER! You are destined to WIN!

Your salvation was not an accident, incident, or coincidence. It was anointed and appointed because He had you on His mind before you were even a thought about or conceived by your parents. While you were yet in your mother's womb, He knew you. You are a child of the Most-High God with a divine appointment to be saved, sanctified, separated, and spared. To God Be the Glory!

In 1 Thessalonians 5:9 – "For God hath not appointed us to wrath, but to obtain salvation by our Lord Jesus Christ." God has set up an established, prearranged way for you and me. Christ was predestined to save you before the foundation of the world. Did you get that? BEFORE the foundation of the world. Well... what is the foundation of the world?

The foundation of the world is, was, and always will be. His Word will forever stand. Even before God spoke a word, your victory was planned and it was personalized. Yet, during the process God was sending prophetic words to confirm what was to be YOUR SALVATION. Your power over the demonic; your strength in times of weakness; your peace in the most turbulent times; your deliverance in the times of darkness, your victory when you feel like you will always be a victim, your hope when you feel all is hopeless; and to top it all off, your blood covenant with the God of Heaven and Earth. All of this was preordained by God; it is unstoppable, unalterable, unchangeable, and irreversible, because He planned it and Jesus' Blood sealed it. Hallelujah! No matter how many times you have been defeated in the past; no matter what the enemy wants to tell you about how you will never experience victory over this area of your life, you forget the past and begin again to expect victory. The Apostle Paul said in Philippians 3:13 "Brethren, I count not myself to have apprehended: but this one thing I do, forgetting those things which are behind, and reaching forth unto those things which are before". Don't allow the enemy to use your past failures to keep you from overcoming now.

Jesus taught us to live one day at a time. "So don't worry about tomorrow, for tomorrow will bring its own worries. Today's trouble is enough for today." (Matthew 6:34, NLT). Don't worry about the days ahead. Stay focused on having victory for today. If you think too far into the future, you will get afraid and might feel defeated before you ever start. Jesus taught us to pray, "Give us this day our daily bread" (Matthew 6:11), and in this He taught us to ask God for what we need for today. God will give you grace and strength one day at a time. I guarantee you that God's love will cover you through it all. I am again a living witness. God knows your heart's desires. You are not a victim, you are Victorious!

Repeat this Prayer: Father, thank You for filling me with your conquering power. I choose to live in faith and declare Your promises over my life. I choose to follow Your Word and stand on the promises from Your Word. I choose Your ways, dear God, knowing that You have good plans for me, in Jesus' name. Amen!

May God's Blessings be upon You!

# SURRENDER IN PEACE

Gizelle Taylor-Daniels
Author, Clinical Office Manager
Family Medical Counseling Service, Pediatrics Department

## ABOUT THE AUTHOR

Gizelle Taylor-Daniels is a wife, a mother of two, and grandmother of two. She is a Clinical Office Manager with the Family Medical Counseling Service (FMCS), Pediatrics Department.

Gizelle is genuinely passionate about helping individuals achieve ultimate health care. She is committed to the promotion of preventive pediatric care. In addition to the promotion of physical, mental, and the social wellbeing of children with the aim of attaining optimal health.

Gizelle enjoys serving her community and her focus has been and will continue to secure maximum results of prosperity and educating the community.

Gizelle holds a B.A. with honors in Health Services and a Certificate as a Community Health Worker from Trinity Washington University.

## CHAPTER 6
## *SURRENDER IN PEACE*

Ten years ago, I desired peace, perfect peace. I wanted freedom from a lifestyle of disturbance that resided within my soul. I desired balance, while my soul desired harmony; I desired to be spiritually healthy and free from fear, doubt, and the past pain.

In the past, I recall family members and friends who spoke highly of God and how peaceful their lives were after surrendering to God. I was aware of God's gift of grace and mercy which He provided daily, but my need from God would be more. As I desired peace, I also knew that my life required a great deal of calm to the many challenging storms in my life.

In my continued meditation, I finally made the decision to surrender to Him and His plan for my life. Although I was no stranger to God, I was fearful of fully submitting to Him. Surrendering to God meant that I had to relinquish all control and my trust to God. I also understood that there was power in relinquishment. We are creatures of habits and choices, and our choices determine our today and our tomorrow. After living a life of heartache, making poor choices, and disappointment after disappointment, I finally realized that life without God was vanity. I knew that my submission to God's authority would provide freedom for me. I made a pledge to myself and to God, to begin to navigate life through His order and direction.

## **FOLLOW YOUR HEART**

Surrendering to God's will was a heart matter. Allowing God to order the steps of my life led me to the beginning of a peaceful heart. I began to feed my spirit and my mind with empowering information daily. I had to change my mindset. Surrounding myself with positive and like-minded individuals who desired God. My hunger and thirst for God became more profound and stronger, and intense. Making this change became my true lifetime of tasting and seeing just how good God is, while understanding that there isn't anything nor anyone in this world that compares, even remotely, to Him.

Matthew 5:6 (NIV) says" Blessed are those who hunger and thirst for righteousness, for they will be filled". It's the greatest blessing to be hungry and thirsty for Jesus; to hunger after the bread of life; and to thirst for living water. I began to appreciate God's Word. By reading and studying God's Word, I discovered how to conform to God's way as well as God's character. Reading and studying the Bible has transformed me.

Prayer is powerful! Prayer is a catalyst; it is like fuel to our lungs with oxygen, and we know that oxygen is our body's life-sustaining gas. I would encourage individuals to develop a disciplined approach to reading God's Word. God's Word leads us to salvation. It is written in His Word that we are saved when we put our hope in Him. Reading the Bible is nourishment to our spirit. God's instruction manual for life is in the Bible. If we focus on His Word and meditate on the Scriptures in the Bible, they will release chains holding us in bondage, and the Word will surely lift our burdens. We gain wisdom, knowledge and understanding when we study the Word. The Scriptures of the Bible will encourage and empower your heart and give hope to your soul when you are facing adversity. You will find peace in the Bible.

## *STRENGTH IN SICKNESS*

As I began to concentrate on the inner work that had begun in me, that is learning about myself through the knowledge of God, this gave me purpose and the desire to become more like Jesus. I was faced with a familiar diagnosis of hypertension (high blood pressure). During my first pregnancy with my eldest son, I started experiencing problems after 20 weeks of pregnancy. I developed high blood pressure and protein in my urine, causing my pressure to be uncontrollable during my pregnancy. I was experiencing elevated levels of protein in my urine (proteinuria), swelling of the hands and feet, headaches that would not go away, and shortness of beath. The elevated blood pressures increased the risk of preeclampsia, preterm birth. Preeclampsia is a serious disorder that can affect all organs in a woman's body. It usually develops after 20 weeks of the pregnancy, often in the third trimester. The preeclampsia prolonged for weeks after the delivery of my eldest son. Preeclampsia caused risk later in my life of kidney disease and continued high blood pressure. While pregnant with my youngest son, secondary to the history of preeclampsia I began to present with similar signs and symptoms which led to preterm birth.

Years later, I was still battling with uncontrolled hypertension (high blood pressure). I recall experiencing severe back pain, swelling of the hands and feet, and shortness of breath. Later in the week the intensity of the back pain was so unbearable, and my shortness of breath had increased. These were all warning signs of an emergency that led me to Washington Hospital Center. Although I am concerned, all the while, I am trying to remain calm. The look that was on my husband's face was a look of grave concern and fear. I began to pray, praying for my healing and with an expectation of being healed. I made calls to family and friends in route to the hospital; I knew that once the calls were made prayer was executed. I also knew that it was essential to keep my faith in God amid the pain and the uncertainty of my health. I remember reminding God of His promises.

With tears rolling down my eyes, I said, Lord you said that you will never leave me nor forsake me. Upon my arrival to Washington Hospital Center, I walked up to the registration desk and stated my name. The staff person looked me in the eyes and said we were expecting you. My Medical Director who I worked with at that time made a call to her goddaughter who was a registered nurse at Washington Hospital Center ER Department, and she told her to take care of me. God's angels were on their assignments and they were truly on their posts, that of intercessory prayers. I was admitted in the hospital for about for 4 days, I was also diagnosed with Stage 3 chronic kidney disease. Stage 3 kidney disease has moderate kidney damage. I gained hope out of a dark moment. I was committed to God and His Word. When you grow in the knowledge of God and your focus is totally on Him, you can, as the Scripture says in 1 Thessalonians 5:18, give thanks in all circumstances, in all things; not for the circumstances, but while going through the circumstances.

## *God, My Protector*

After being diagnosed with Stage 3 kidney disease I had to rebuild my life. Living with a chronic illness required God's Word and His comfort toward me. Chronic illnesses produce exhaustion, fear, guilt, and sometimes resentment. Feelings of frustration and sadness, the changes in our self-esteem concerning our physical appearance and body image issues can all arise at some point or another while living with a chronic disease. I have been very fortunate to have a great support system in addition to an awesome, very wise and knowledgeable Nephrologist. My husband and I have been blessed by God's protection.

God led both my husband and I to knowledgeable and well capable physicians who provided me continuity of care. While the physicians provided physical care, God continued to heal my soul spiritually. Today, I am stable living with Stage 3 kidney disease. My new life's mission is to provide preventive care to every infant, toddler, and adolescent that I encounter at Family and Medical Counseling Service Inc. I will raise awareness, advocate, and provide continuity of care for my community. I gained insight during my struggles with Stage 3 kidney disease. I learned that God's ways are higher than our ways. God was my strength and my refuge. God made me in His image. I am fearfully and wonderfully made!!! God has been with me since the beginning and will continue to see me through. I developed a friendship with God through my many seasons of both good and bad. Remember, when thou pass through the waters, I will be with thee; and through the rivers, they shall not overflow thee; when thou walk through the fire, thou shalt not be burned; neither shall the flame kindle upon thee. You see, we are never alone. The Bible assures us that God is present, protecting us, and revealing unto us our safety in the Spirit.

## GOD'S CLARITY

As a result of God's protection, I began to focus on my spiritual vision. For many years I was functioning and navigating through life with tunnel vision. However, I wasn't aware of my giftings from God, but I was aware of my empathy for others. I would always find joy and peace in serving others as well. I could not understand why tragic news would sadden me in a way that would cause me to really become really troubled, and more importantly, the individual could be a stranger and I would be saddened because of their tragedy. I would pray for all; the strangers I met, their families, relatives, and friends, for comfort, strength and sometimes healing. The emotions that I often felt were unclear to me. I recall sharing my emotions with my sister, who informed me that I was operating in the capacity of an intercessor. Praying was something I was familiar with. The term intercessory prayer was new to me. Prayer, is speaking to God, having a one on one communication with God. Intercession involves standing in the gap, an intervention, stepping in on somebody else's behalf through prayer. This is something that I do on a regular basis. I began to seek out Scriptures about intercessory prayer for true clarity. I also learned that intercession is a gift that God provides.

I continued to be passionate about having clarity of my spiritual vision. It was important that I receive clarification from God. I was very passionate about serving others, encouraging individuals, and educating my community in the capacity of reaching our full potential in Christ. My vision became my life, and my purpose. I remember praying to God for confirmation. God provided confirmation to me by way of a dream. This is how God communicates with me and He has placed on my heart for the manifestation of answered prayers, to come to pass. My vision and my purpose are both unique and God has placed them in my heart. Clarity for your journey in life begins and ends with Jesus. There are no limits on the vision and clarity that God brings into our lives. As I began to take steps in the direction of my purpose, I asked God to provide me with His wisdom.

## *Surrendering to His Wisdom*

Having godly wisdom means we strive to see life from God's perspective and act accordingly. The Book of Proverbs in the Old Testament of the Bible is known as wisdom literature. Proverbs is full of practical instructions for life. The beginning of the instructions is mentioned first in Genesis 1:26, "And God said, let us make man in our image, after our likeness and let them have dominion over the fish of the sea, and over the fowl of the air, and over the cattle, and over all the earth, and over every creeping thing that creepeth upon the earth." The word dominion stands out to me. To have dominion over something or someone we must have knowledge. Dominion represents control or power, or the authority to rule. In continuing to step into my purpose, I continued to seek God for His guidance. Now I started seeking God's wisdom because I no longer want to lean to my own understanding. The pattern of my ways is not necessarily working in my favor. In fact, I was lacking wisdom during the health challenges of my life. To experience life as God intended righteously, we need His wisdom to act accordingly. An individual could have righteousness and a pure heart but lack wisdom. With wisdom we can maintain what we have obtained from God.

There is a saying that "when you are given lemons in life, make lemonade". My goal was to use God's wisdom to arrive to the next level of my life the life God created for me. I wanted to operate as a game changer. I no longer wanted to allow my emotions to dictate my life and or responses to adversity. However, I wanted to use my emotions as an indicator to adjust and correct my behavior before any negative exposure. I wanted to walk in wisdom, Godly Wisdom, discernment, and faith always. So, I begin to read and study the Book of Proverbs seeking verses that would allow me to gain emotional, cultural, and spiritual development through wise counsel. I received the instructions, and I began to operate in wise behavior. I began to build my house on a solid rock of truth and never to look back. My exposure to God's wisdom was so profound. I realized that ignorance and suffering were no longer the road to travel. Truly, God's wisdom is the way!!!

## PEACE AND FLOURISHING

Life is seasonal, that is life is seasons for change, growth, and renewal. According to Oxford Dictionary the word flourishing is defined as developing rapidly and successfully, thriving, if you will. When I made the decision to surrender to God, I decided to reach a height of development and or influence. In the beginning, my transformation mirrored the pupa stage of a caterpillar. The pupa stage is when the caterpillar's old body dies and a new body forms inside a protective shell known as the chrysalis, the caterpillar is transforming into a new creature. I went through a life cycle that involved several stages just like a butterfly. I experienced four stages during my life cycle surrendering my heart, surrendering my spirit, surrendering my soul, and finally surrendering to God. The Bible says that anyone who belongs to Christ has become a new creation. My old life was gone, and the new life had begun. The same God who took a caterpillar and changed it into a butterfly, transformed a sinner into a saint.

The transformation of a butterfly teaches us that change takes time and can be a little difficult in the beginning, but the end results are beautiful. There's value, and power in relinquishment of the old, to develop into the new. I embraced the growth, patience and perseverance, adaptation, and faith. I once read a quote that stated "A season of loneliness and isolation is when the caterpillar gets its wings. Remember that next time you feel alone", – Mandy Hale. Here's another quote that states, "Butterflies can't see their wings. They can't see how truly beautiful they are, but everyone else can. People are like that as well". – Naya Rivera.

## **THE VICTORY IN SURRENDER**

*My Prayer:* "Father, I acknowledge that You are worthy of all honor, glory, and praise. I am thankful for the victorious work of Your Son, Jesus, at Calvary for me. I claim His victory for myself now as I willingly surrender every area of my life to Your will". God truly blessed me with peace, spiritual peace, and the Prince of Peace daily. I was a hurting woman and seeking after God's heart and I discovered peace amid pain, brokenness, and uncertainty. I surrendered and God took care of the rest. I have always been that individual who wanted to control my life. I always wanted to be married without children, I wanted to attend college to pursue a degree in law. My dream car was a Mercedes Benz 2 Door Sports model. I had always wanted to travel, broaden my horizon, go on adventures for the wonderful exposure and the experience, and when I put my trust in God and surrendered to Him, they all happened.

I just celebrated my ten-year anniversary. I am married to my soul mate, and I am the mother of two handsome young men and a grandmother of two beautiful grandchildren. I am a Clinical Office Manager of a pediatric clinic within my community. Four years ago, I was presented with the opportunity to obtain my A.A. in Professional Studies at Trinity Washington University. I completed the two-year degree program with honors and decided to continue furthering my education. I hold a B.A. with honors in Health Services in addition to a Certificate in Community Health Worker from Trinity Washington University. God opened many doors and changed my life. I am humbled by God's goodness. So, I leave you with this: "Trust in the Lord with all thine heart; and lean not unto thine own understanding. In all thy ways acknowledge him, and he shall direct thy paths". Proverbs 3:5-6 (KJV)

# HEALED AND FREE

Elder Felicia Edmond
Amazon International Bestselling Author,
Speaker, Coach
Host of Breakthrough to Your Next Level Podcast

## ABOUT THE AUTHOR

Elder Felicia Edmond is a minister, an Amazon International Bestselling Author, Speaker, Coach and Radio Host. Felicia has a passion for caring and seeing people encounter breakthroughs and freedom in areas where they are challenged and receive the love of God. She lives by the fact that God has created each of us uniquely and we can discover our God given gifts as we seek Him. Felicia is the author of *Breakthrough Book of Poems and Prayers*. Felicia is a contributing author in Visionary Author Reverend Allison G. Daniel's Anthology: *Empowered to Win 2* Felicia's chapter is Depression to Destiny.

Felicia is married to her husband Jerry; they have two beautiful children, Joelle and Jonathan. Along with her husband, they both serve as elders in her home church where she enjoys serving, preaching, and teaching the Gospel of Jesus Christ.

Felicia has a Bachelor of Science Degree in Accounting from Hampton University, and a Master of Counseling from Trinity University.

## Chapter 7
## Healed and Free

*Galatians 5:1 "Stand fast therefore in the liberty wherewith Christ hath made us free, and be not entangled again with the yoke of bondage."*

The bondage of rejection began to permeate my life and the decisions that I made from a young age. I endured trauma and bullying in my young childhood, as many have endured. I began to become withdrawn and hidden. The result was that I began to develop a fear of rejection. I took on perfectionism and made decisions throughout life at times to gain acceptance. My self-esteem was impacted negatively. As I surrendered my life to Christ, I began to understand the acceptance and love Christ had for me. I knew deep down inside that Christ loved me and died for me. However, I still had the overwhelming shadow of rejection hovering over me.

I began to embark upon marriage, family, career and serving in ministry. By God's grace, I was able to gain success in many areas of my life. Through God's personal leading and His guidance for me, I became a stay-at-home mother. As I became a stay-at-home mom, I focused on family but also desired ministry and career. After encountering a state of depression and my attempt to overcome it daily as God delivered me, I decided to launch out fully into ministry. However, and unfortunately, I endured rejection in ministry head on, ultimately leading me to a deeper bout with depression. On several occasions, I was told I was unqualified because I had a quiet demeanor. It's unfortunate, that many times people will view or focus on you from the outside and they are unable or cannot see the gifts God has placed within you –on the inside. Sometimes people are unable to see how God can use us as His vessels because of how we may appear to them. We must remember that it is God who works in us both to will and to do of His good pleasure according to Philippians 2:13. One may appear quiet on the outside or look unqualified to man on the outside, but when the anointing of the Lord is upon the person, he or she can fully operate in the gifts that God has placed on the inside. Despite the words and negative comments and reactions regarding my call to ministry, I was persuaded by God concerning His call to continue to minister to others and preach the Gospel. I knew on the inside what God had called me to do. As the prophet Jeremiah says, it was like fire shut up in my bones. I had to speak forth the Word of God!

Now with excitement and eagerness to share God's Word to the multitude, I began with becoming an author and a speaker and I thoroughly enjoyed stepping into my purpose and calling. When I began to move in my purpose, the process of healing began, from years of bondage to rejection. Healing from rejection can be a daily process because the enemy attacks in the area of rejection in a myriad of different ways. It takes a daily standing on God's Word, putting on the whole armor of God and totally trusting Him. My healing process began with my staying in His presence, staying in His Word and thereby understanding true love, true forgiveness and casting down imaginations.

I had to become present before the Lord and to be still and know that He is God. During this time of staying in God's presence, He began to give me revelation about experiencing freedom. God helped me to see that I am not rejected, because He has accepted me in the beloved. He has chosen me, which means He has selected and handpicked me, specifically, to do what He has called me to do.

1 Peter 2:9 (ESV) says "But you are a chosen race, a royal priesthood, a holy nation, a people for his own possession, that you may proclaim the excellencies of him who called you out of darkness into his marvelous light." He has selected me on purpose. If God be for me, who can be against me. My identity is found in Christ alone because Christ has accepted my true identity – it's His acceptance that truly matters. He placed on my heart to stand and look in the mirror and begin to realize that I am

fearfully and wonderfully made. He heals every wound. By His stripes I am healed. Who the Son has set free –is free indeed, so God had me face the fact that although I encountered rejection (and all will encounter rejection at some point in life), but this will never change about how God feels about me. James 1:17 says "Every good gift and every perfect gift is from above, and cometh down from the Father of lights, with whom is no variableness, neither shadow of turning." God never changes and He loves us with an everlasting love. We know that His favor surrounds us like a shield. God will also send the right people in our lives to appreciate the real us, and who we are in Him. God is faithful and this is what began happening in my life. He began surrounding me with like-minded people who appreciated the call of God on my life.

Once I began to wholeheartedly focus, and I stayed in God's presence, and truly knew who He has created me to be, my next step was to begin to understand true forgiveness. I had to learn that there is true freedom in forgiveness. Colossians 3:13 (NKJV) says "bearing with one another, and forgiving one another, if anyone has a complaint against another; even as Christ forgave you, so you also must do."

Forgiveness means to pardon, releasing the individual from punishment. We are releasing the person; we are not saying that what was done was right. I am learning through the process of forgiveness, as I have come to realize just how much Christ loves and forgives me. My forgiveness for others comes out of the overflow of the love and forgiveness that Christ has for me. I realized that I now had the grace to forgive, in spite of hurt and disappointment. Hebrews 4 reminds us that we can come boldly to the throne of grace, that we may obtain mercy and find grace to help in time of need. God's grace can help us through hurt and disappointment, as we forgive. Through God's mercy and the encouragement of a Christian mentor, I began to develop practical ways to assist in the forgiveness process. I began to release hurt, through journaling and writing letters, to the person that I would not send. The letters indicated my authentic emotions and hurt and ended with kind words regarding the person. This journaling and letters were for my personal healing. I wanted to release any emotions that were buried on the inside of me so that healing could begin. I did not desire to hold on to hurt and unforgiveness, which can turn to bitterness and as I released people as God led me to release, I began to experience peace. The forgiveness process is a continuous process with Christ. We are constantly in a state of applying forgiveness to our lives as various situations occur.

In addition to being consistently and continually in

God's presence, and the forgiving process, I had to cast down negative thoughts and imaginations about myself. I realized that my thoughts and imaginations had, ultimately, turned into strongholds developed through the years. 2 Corinthians 10:4-5 (NKJV) says "For the weapons of our warfare are not carnal but mighty in God for pulling down strongholds, casting down arguments and every high thing that exalts itself against the knowledge of God, bringing every thought into captivity to the obedience of Christ,". After many years of taking on the identity that I was rejected and then further being rejected in ministry, I had to bring every thought captive. You see, my thought was that I was not good enough. I would resist the negative thought and replace it with I am fearfully and wonderfully made. People would sometimes say that I was timid and, subsequently, they would overlook what I had to say or share. God says has He has not given me the spirit of fear but power love and a sound mind. The enemy will oftentimes tell us that people don't like you, but God's Word says His favor surrounds me as a shield. Once we realize and know with confidence from God's Word, that is –His standards –that we are not to wrestle against flesh and blood, only then can we recognize and know that these are the lies of the enemy. God truly loves us and wants us to live an abundant life in Him. We shall know the truth and the truth shall make us free. So then, I began to recognize and appreciate that Jesus purchased my freedom on the cross. Therefore, I am already free, and I cannot be entangled in the yolk of bondage. We must understand that truly, it is a daily process. Yes, rejection will come, and yes, we will experience hurt and disappointments, even at times and/or from the person or individuals we least expect. However, each day, we are persuaded that we are not alone, and that nothing can separate us from God's love. We have a loving Savior Jesus the Christ, who will never leave us nor forsake us. He has justified and redeemed us so that we can glorify His name. Every time the rejection comes, or the thought comes, we must remember that we have the victory in Christ Jesus. Luke 10:19 (NKJV) says "Behold, I give you the authority to trample on serpents and scorpions, and over all the power of the enemy, and nothing shall by any means hurt you." He has given us authority to cast negative thoughts and imaginations down.

The steps of being continually and consistently in God's presence, and meditating on His Word through my process, thereby releasing forgiveness and casting down negative imaginations, has, without a doubt, been key to my deliverance. God showed me that He always has a higher plan and purpose. According to Isaiah 55:9 (NIV) "As the heavens are higher than the earth, so are my ways higher than your ways and my thoughts than your thoughts." Sometimes rejection from others is God's way of moving us into having a greater and higher experience in Him. God moved me from holding on to the spirit of rejection and into ministry, to fulfill His designed purpose for me. By the grace of God, I am now freely preaching the Gospel as I was called to do. God knows me intimately and He called me before I was in my mother's womb. No one could not stop the purpose of God in my life if I did not allow or permit them. It is vital to walk in our purpose because there are specific individuals who God has called us to reach. There are assignments that we must fulfill as God leads. We cannot consider the rejection from others in making our decision to follow the will of God. Man looks at the outward appearance, however and glory to God, He looks at the heart. God truly cares about our hearts and our love for Him and for others. God wants to be our only source and our refuge, and we are not to dwell on the opinion of others to be our source. Psalm 118:8 says it is better to trust in the Lord than to put confidence in man. God is the one who truly places us in our true purpose. Each day is a new day to walk out our purpose. God gives us another chance each day that we wake up because He is faithful, and His mercies are new every morning. Although there are challenging days that we will encounter, I must, continuously, remind myself of who God says I am and continuously realize the power of forgiveness as I bask in the presence of God. Now, I can stand boldly in my identity in Christ, and I can minister to others with freedom. For me, my freedom and answering God's call on my life, I believe, was and could have been the catalyst in assisting someone in their deliverance and freedom. I now choose daily to not be entangled again in the yolk of bondage. I had to make this choice each day as challenges came, and from time to time, will still come. I know that Jesus purchased my freedom and I know that He has given me the power to walk in His grace and this abundant life, in Him. Because of Jesus, and His shed blood for me, I am healed, and I am free.

## **REFLECTION QUESTIONS**

1. Has there ever been a time in your life wherein you experienced rejection, and if so, how did you overcome it?
2. Is there a time in your life where you might have been in bondage toward something or someone, or experienced unforgiveness on your part or from another, and if so, what steps did you take towards your freedom?
3. Currently, now, is there an area in your life that you recognize that God wants you to experience freedom in and, if so, what will be the first step you will take toward your freedom?

# UNBECOMING TO BECOME

Reverend Suzette Hampton
Author, Founder of Trees of Righteousness
(TOR) Women's Ministry

## ABOUT THE AUTHOR

Reverend Suzette Hampton, born and raised in the Washington Metropolitan area, is a minister, realtor, entrepreneur, author, mother of four (4), and grandmother of eight (8).

From an early age, she was taught the value and honor of serving others and brings this core value to bear in every area of her life. She serves in various capacities with hard work, integrity, and dedication.

One of her favorite quotes:

> "Life's most persistent and urgent question is, 'What are you doing for others?'"
> –Martin Luther King, Jr.

Reverend Hampton is the founder of the Trees of Righteousness (TOR) Women's Ministry, where she encourages, empowers, and strengthens women to their full potential in God by providing opportunities for spiritual growth and development, meaningful fellowship, and a welcoming, safe, and supportive environment in which to confront and be healed from spiritual, mental, and emotional pain and trauma. She is very actively involved in her community and is particularly passionate about assisting the homeless in her immediate area and the DMV arena.

# Chapter 8
## Unbecoming to Become

It was 2017, and the first few days of summer still felt like spring. From the outside looking in, my life appeared to be great. What no one knew, however, was that I was struggling on the inside. I felt empty, alone, stagnant, and stuck. I needed help and I needed it desperately. I cried out to God, and He instructed me to reach out to a particular person to request counseling. Despite my skepticism, I followed His instruction. My obedience saved my life.

By all accounts, I should have been happy. I had a great job, beautiful, healthy children and grandchildren, and a network of supportive and loving family and close friends. Unfortunately, none of that prevented me from experiencing the despondency and desperation that seemed to swell on the inside of me. I was in church every Sunday and at Bible study every Wednesday, but I was also in pain and very aware of the brokenness inside. I was familiar with pain because I had felt it for most of my life. In fact, I had experienced pain on so many different levels that I'd almost become numb to it. However, this pain was different. I knew that I had to get help soon or I was going to die and that's exactly what I told the person who agreed to be my counselor.

At the time, I was following a pattern that had been established early in my life. I took care of people, I served others, and I put everyone else's needs before my own, failing to think of myself outside of my basic needs. I was a mother, grandmother, daughter, sister, friend, minister, and supervisor. I was an expert at functioning in each one of those capacities – being and doing everything for everyone. At the end of the day, however, there was little to nothing left for me. I did the one thing I knew to do which was to pray. I asked the Lord to help me, to heal me and deliver me. I asked Him to reveal whatever was going on inside me that was displeasing to Him or that was a hindrance to my spiritual growth and well-being. I asked Him to expose everything that prevented me from being able to love myself.

Back then, I believed that I was self-aware. I thought that I practiced self-examination. In all honesty, I had no real idea of who I was or what I wanted. I didn't know that I'd lived in a state of depression for years. I didn't know why I was so angry or what to do about it. I didn't know how to bring about the change I so desperately needed.

The person to whom God sent me for counseling was a Christian and a minister, like me. She was very reluctant to counsel me and, in fact, told me no when I initially asked. However, I was sure that the Lord had sent me to her, so I told her to speak with Him about it and let me know when we'd be able to get started. The next day, we scheduled my first counseling session. We made sure to keep God first – at the forefront of everything we did. We prayed before and after each session, prayed about each assignment, and sought God for guidance and direction.

My first counseling session was extremely challenging. I was asked to answer questions about myself that were uncomfortable, to think and speak about things that were both painful and frightening. I was initially very concerned about whether I'd be able to follow through with it. I didn't know if I was strong enough or brave enough. My counselor encouraged me to commit to the process and do the work that needed to be done so that I could be freed from the issues that had plagued me for so long. I was terrified but I knew that it was necessary if I truly wanted to be healed. I learned so much about myself during counseling.

For example,
- I learned that there was much more brokenness inside me than I understood.
- I learned that I had not fully dealt with the sexual abuse I had been a victim of as a child.
- I learned that I was so fiercely protective of others because I had not been protected as a child.
- I learned that I was codependent and that I

attracted needy people because I needed to be needed.
- I learned that there was a scared, broken little girl inside of me for whom I had not properly cared.
- I learned that I was angry with myself for repeatedly letting myself and others down.
- I learned that, although I held myself to a higher standard than everyone else, I didn't believe I was worthy or deserving of anything good.
- I learned that I minimized myself, in order to make others feel comfortable.

These realizations (and others) triggered a defense mechanism called avoidance that I had developed during my childhood. I had always avoided confrontations, difficult conversations, and anything else that might possibly cause me pain or make me uncomfortable. The pain from facing my truths was SO intense that I frequently cried out to the Lord for the ability to be consistent and remain committed to the process. I cried more during the 18 months of counseling than I had in my previous 10 years! I cried so much that, sometimes, there were no tears left and all I could do was moan.

One of the most memorable assignments I was given in counseling was having to ask 5 people who knew me well (and whom I trusted) to share with me their views/opinions of me. My lack of self-esteem was so pronounced that the thought of completing the assignment caused immediate fear and anxiety which, in turn, almost shut me down. I remember dropping my head, fighting back tears, and taking deep breaths to calm myself. As I worked through the assignment, I began to realize some of the reasons why I felt such resistance. They were...

- I didn't want anyone to lie to me, in order to keep from hurting my feelings.
- I was afraid of hearing positive things about myself that I knew I didn't and wouldn't believe.
- Understanding that others loved me more than I loved myself was VERY painful.

Although I was full of dread, I eventually made a commitment to myself and my counselor to do it. I remember typing and retyping the email because I was having such a difficult time explaining what I needed in a way that didn't seem selfish or prideful to me. Even though everyone I asked was someone I knew, loved, and trusted, I was so worried that they would view me in a negative light and receive the request in a way other than the original intent. I beat myself up with negative self-talk which only made the assignment even less desirable than it already was.

At my next session, I was required to read the responses – OUT LOUD! It wasn't enough for me to read what people thought of me. I had to hear myself reading it!! It was nearly impossible for me to do, and I cried the entire time! Their words were both painful and comforting at the same time. How could someone believe me to be strong when I felt so weak? How could someone think I was phenomenal or charismatic or brave? Then I thought, 'Wait, someone thinks I'm wise? Someone else believes I'm fearless?' These were people I knew, people I trusted, intelligent people. I had to believe that there was some truth to what they were saying.

Over the next 18 months, as we peeled back more layers, I continued to cry out to God. I journaled my way through the entire process and, sometimes, it felt like I would never be healed. But God is SO faithful. He wouldn't let me quit and neither would my counselor. The Lord gave me the courage and strength I needed to keep going, to persevere in order to strip away all the lies I had believed. He gave me the power to begin the process of unbecoming!

The Lord also gave me what I didn't know I needed – someone with whom I could take the journey! Within the first few sessions, my counselor and I discovered what neither of us knew when we initially started. We discovered that God, in His omniscience, was using my sessions to heal both of us! Each assignment I was given to complete, my counselor committed to completing as well. We were amazed by the multitude of ways that God carried out His purpose for each of us. We were grateful for each stage of the healing process.

As my knowledge of and love for God increased, so did my knowledge of and love for myself. I began to see myself the way God sees me and to believe about myself what the Word says about me – that I am chosen, that I am redeemed, that I am free from the law of sin and death, that I am the righteousness of God in Christ Jesus. I came to understand that my worth, my value, is not found in man. My value can only be found in God! In essence, I began the journey of becoming the woman I was created to be.

As I healed, I was also very eager to spend more time in the Word. I was rewarded for doing so with several reminders from the Lord.

- I was reminded that the Lord meets us right where we are. Revelation 3:20 says 'Behold, I stand at the door, and knock: if any man hear my voice, and open the door, I will come in to him, and will sup with him, and he with me.'
- I was reminded that He loves us way too much to allow us to stay stuck. 1 John 3:1 says 'Behold, what manner of love the Father hath bestowed

upon us, that we should be called the sons of God: ...'
- I was reminded that, with God, nothing is wasted! Romans 8:28 says '... all things work together for good to them that love God, to them who are the called according to his purpose.'
- I was reminded that He uses people, things, circumstances, and situations that most people would see no value in. 1 Corinthians 1:27 says 'But God has chosen the foolish things of the world to confound the wise; ...'
- I was reminded that there is purpose in everything!

I learned many, many valuable lessons during counseling but there were two very specific instructions from the Lord that I've followed since then. The first was to 'learn to love the process.' He impressed upon me to stop resisting the process of change simply because it was scary or uncomfortable or even painful. He instructed me to change the way I viewed the process – to view it as the road to healing and peace, to see it as my way out, to cooperate with it in order to expedite it. The second lesson was 'to surrender.' Now, this initially seemed like a simple instruction, but I learned that it is far more involved than what most people think or understand. Surrender isn't simply giving up or letting go of myself.

It means 'to give oneself up into the power of another.' It means that I must give up what I want, what I think is right, what I believe, and what I feel in order to allow what God wants for me! It means that God's will (for me and everyone else) is best and I must yield to it. It also means letting go of the outcome! I learned that surrender is a lifestyle and not simply a one-time event. It must be practiced because it is contrary to what our flesh desires. However, the benefits are out of this world!!

I've always been very sensitive and compassionate to hurting women, so I started a women's ministry in 2010. As God guided me through MY healing process, my desire to help others through their healing process increased exponentially! I refocused my efforts on creating a safe and supportive environment where women were able to express, acknowledge, accept, and heal from their own hurt, pain, brokenness, and experiences. I shared my experiences from a place of authenticity and encouraged others to do the same. I shared the truths (the good, the bad, and the ugly) that were revealed to me about myself and the lessons I learned during the process. I shared the depths of love, compassion, and faithfulness God showered upon me during the process and how frequently I rested in Him.

As I continue to unbecome what I was never meant to be, I am still becoming the woman God created me to be. I am blessed with many opportunities to minister to women individually and collectively, to help them along their own journey of unbecoming to become. I'm so very honored to be trusted with this responsibility and I totally depend on the Lord to help me do so.

# WINNING BEGINS WITHIN

Minister Cathy Henderson
Consultant, Trainer, Certified Transformation Coach
Founder & Executive Director, Up Empowerment, Inc.
www.cathyhglobal.com

## ABOUT THE AUTHOR

Pastor Cathy Henderson, native of Charlotte, North Carolina is a Consultant, Trainer, Certified Transformation Coach and Minister. A prolific and thought-provoking speaker, Cathy delivers in dynamic and diverse ways in both business and Christian arenas.

Cathy is a servant-lover of God! She was ordained in 2005 and currently pastors a church plant. She is passionate about advancing the Kingdom of God and equipping the people of God. She views all her work as an extension of ministry.

In business, Cathy has 20+ years of management in behavioral and public health with a career-long reputation as a catalyst for change and synergy. She has been recognized for winning communication, program development, and collaborative relationship-building. She is founder and Executive Director of Up Empowerment, Inc, a non-profit organization which helps individuals, families and communities unlock their God-given potential, increase impact, and build legacy.

Cathy carries a charisma-borne passion for life and a compassion for people.

One of her greatest joys is seeing people experience a

"light bulb" moment where they have a revelation about their situation, which gives them clarity and provokes positive change.

# CHAPTER 9
# WINNING BEGINS WITHIN

It all started when I was in high school. I felt derailed. There was a path before me, but I did not feel connected to it. So, what did I do? I fought it! I rebelled against it! I teetered on the edge of the path...one foot on the path, and the other foot off. I had options for attending college. I received acceptance to three colleges, with scholarships, in the first quarter (October) of my senior year, but I almost flunked out and just barely graduated! Wait...what? Prior to my senior year, I was a high performing student, a member of the honor society, and in the top 5% of my class. During my senior year, I let it all go! I began missing, or rather skipping classes, if you will, and not turning in my assignments; just going through the motions but not really getting anything accomplished. It had gotten so bad that my teachers who had known me over the years, were concerned. They asked what was wrong with me and they even covered for me. My English teacher gave (I do mean gave) me a "D" because if he had given the "F" I'd earned, I would not have graduated. He told me that he knew I was more than capable and that whatever I had going on, he could not allow me to fail myself, and he was not giving me an excuse to not take my scholarship.

## LOCATE YOURSELF

Think about this: You have a clear path; you are capable of accomplishing the assignments and tasks, and there is a reward ahead for you...but the will to get the assignments and tasks done, is totally absent.

- Have you ever experienced this?
- Do you have an area in your life going like this right now?

So, I made it! I entered college with a full scholarship. All is well, right? Well, it happened again in college. Again, I felt derailed. I could not nail down why I was there, that is, what I wanted to study. First it was Biology because I thought I wanted to be a doctor. But then I decided I didn't want to be in school that long, so I changed my major to Chemistry. This would get me admitted to the nursing program, and I'd become a nurse anesthetist. But then I decided I didn't want to do nursing, so I changed my major to Communication Sciences because I wanted to be a speech language pathologist. But, nope, changed my mind again. I finally landed on Psychology and decided that this was it. By now it was second semester of my junior year, and I started losing interest in school. So, what did I do? Yep, I started fighting the path before me! I rebelled against it! I started missing classes and doing last minute work. I was placed on academic probation, and I almost lost my scholarships. After an intervention and strong "encouragement" from my parents I pulled it together enough to get by. It meant adding an extra semester to make up for the semesters I flubbed! Although I graduated, with honors, it didn't feel significant to me.

## LOCATE YOURSELF

Unclear path...unsure of yourself...not connected to what is going on or what you're doing with and in your life.

- Have you had a repeated cycle of disruption, disconnect or derailment?
- Have you moved passed it but not felt successful?
- Are you still waiting for the "big connect?"

I started my first job after college as the director of an academy that provided after school and summer camp programs, however, I still wasn't sure what I wanted to do; I just wanted to start working. Then something amazing happened. I realized I had a "knack" for managing children and for sharing tips with their parents to address behavioral and academic performance. I started looking and applying for jobs related to teaching parents. When I received a call to interview with our local school system for a parent-educator role, I was shocked, but pleased. I walked in the door, saw an interview panel of seven people, and began quaking inwardly! What was

I, a 23-year-old with no children, going to say to these people about why they should hire me to educate parents? I took a deep breath, said an inward prayer, and then opened my mouth to answer their questions. It was in that moment that I knew this was an assignment from God. I've come to realize that when God is giving the assignment, He has already equipped us to complete it. I got the job! As I embraced the assignment, I leaned into my assets, my strengths. I discovered that speaking to crowds, problem solving, and connecting with people were my innate strengths. No one taught me to do these things, but I realized that they had been showing up in my life since I was a small child. I became a sought-after parenting educator, doing workshops at over 40 schools and pre-k centers and providing individual parenting education to hundreds of parents.

Now you might ask, how was I bold enough to move in this manner when I didn't have any real experience (via my own children) or education (via child development, adult education, etc.)? It was God's assignment for me. I understood that my innate assets made me suited. As I used the assets God placed within me, I had many opportunities to sharpen my skills, learn through others' experiences and attain professional certifications. It happened as I went.

## **LOCATE YOURSELF**

- Are there endeavors or goals in your life that you want to reach but haven't because you believe you don't have the skills?
- Do you sense that God has an assignment for you in a particular area? If so, what assets (gifts and talents) do you possess that align with the assignment?
- What is in you that you need to bring forward and move in?
- As you move in your assets, what opportunities await you to sharpen your skills and position you for maximum success?

Now, let's talk about progression and the uncovering of your gifts and talents within. While I was working for the school system, a leader from a non-profit agency providing services to abused and neglected children heard me facilitating a workshop and approached me about contracting with their agency. So, I began working with them and I quickly realized that there were changes that could be made to their processes to increase the effectiveness of their parenting program. This was my innate ability to solve problems that businesses and organizations may encounter. I took their current process, tweaked it, added to it, created standardized approaches and forms, and assisted the family educators on staff in implementing the new approach for the program. In case it wasn't clear from my first job, another of my innate strengths is leadership. I am a leader and an influencer. While I was contracting, a Senior Family Educator position became available, and they asked me if I would join the staff full-time in that position. I did! Within nine months of leading as the Senior Family Educator, I applied for and became the Manager of Family Education. Within two years, I had increased the program's services and contracts and expanded the program to two additional counties. Additionally, I took on two new departments and pioneered a new therapeutic unit. What happened? You guessed it; I progressed, sharpened my skills, and obtained additional certifications. Most importantly, I uncovered another strength...that I am a pioneer! The ability to easily start new endeavors and build upon them from the ground up is innate. I realized that I was able to approach jobs and interviews, no matter whether I qualified ON PAPER or not, because I knew I could do it and I had no fear of the unknown or accomplishing something new.

## LOCATE YOURSELF

- Can you find yourself in this?
- As you think about your life, are you able to identify progression?
- Even if you didn't realize it before now, can you

> see the uncovering of assets within you over time?

I've talked about my assets, strengths, and skills, right? I mean I made it sound very easy to embrace them and accept my assignments, right? I even implied ease at increasing my abilities through experience and training. Ummm, it wasn't ALL easy! Honestly, I really grazed over my abilities. Abilities are valuable skills that are learned and applied. I am STILL increasing my abilities by learning new skills and increasing the level of mastery with older skills. While I have many wonderful assets (leadership, pioneering, problem solving, etc.), I've learned that I am more visionary; able to look at the big picture and hold intensity around the start of a project. Beyond that, I must work at my skills around the details...e.g., prioritizing tasks, deadlines, pacing my assignments (read this as not procrastinating), and long term interest (sometimes I'm ready to move to the next new thing). I also must lean on the skills of others by delegating (which is a skill) and trusting others to run with the vision. Oh, and guess what else...I started THREE different graduate school programs (hangs head, but no shame). One more....AND I stopped the final program for almost a year before God convicted me and told me to FINISH it. Why am I telling you this? Because even with these hiccups, I'm still successful and I'm still fulfilling my God given assignments because I keep acting on the assets within me. You know what, you can too! Don't be down on yourself because you lack ability, just open yourself to learn and grow. There are so many resources to increase our skills. There are books, free information on the internet and YouTube. There are free and paid courses on just about any and everything! Don't limit what you have within (your assets) or miss your assignment from God just because your skills (abilities) aren't yet developed or sharpened!

I must note here that while my assets were being uncovered, I also had to deal with the experiences that led to my feeling derailed and repeating unproductive cycles. If our assets are unacknowledged or we experience difficulties, failures, or trauma in our formative years as children and young adults, our assets can lie dormant, covered with pain, insecurities, fear of rejection, fear of failure and the like. We must do the difficult work of healing those inner wounds and breaking out of the altered self that we adapt to because of our challenging experiences. I talk more about this process in my March 2022 book release on allies and adversaries of destiny.

In a teaching by Myles Monroe, he talks about a tree seed. He says that inside the seed, is a tree and inside the tree are the leaves and anything else the tree will produce (blooms and fruits). We are like that; we came from the seed of a man and when we were planted in our mothers' wombs as an embryo, our adult self was already there (Psalms 139:16). God has wired us and given us assets or innate strengths that He expects us to use and cultivate to produce fruit so that others can benefit from them.

Know this, while you're acting on your assets, sharpening your abilities, accepting God's assignments, life is still happening! You will still miss it sometimes. Through it all, your inner assets are greater than what you go through. God's assignments for you are greater than the obstacles in front of you. What God has placed in you is more powerful than the adversaries trying to come against you. Though challenges will come, don't give up! What is in you is valuable and necessary. You are empowered to win...connect with God and use your assets within!

## **ASSETS**

- What are your assets?
- What valuable qualities and strengths do you naturally possess?
- What assets do you have that are under expressed?
- Which of these asset(s) would you like to see used more?

## **ABILITIES**

- What valuable skills have you developed over time?
- What do you know how to do?
- What do you know the ins and outs of?
- Which skills noted are underutilized?
- Which skills above do you find pleasure in?
- Which skills above do you have but don't find pleasure in?
- What skills are you interested in but have not explored?

## **ACTION**

- What actions do you need to take now to pull your assets, abilities, and assignments together and move forward?

# LEARNING TO LOVE THE GIFT – ME!

Pastor Valerie Howard-Jones
CEO of Pastor Val Ministries,
CEO, Sister I've Been There Too Literary Group
Director of Pastoral Counseling and Prayer for I AM My Sister's Keeper

## ABOUT THE AUTHOR

Valerie M. Howard-Jones is a DC native, and she currently resides in Glenn Dale, MD. She is the CEO of Pastor Val Ministries.

Pastor Val, as she is affectionately called, was licensed to preach the Gospel in 1994 by Bishop Kevin V. Gresham, Sr., of the Greater St. John Church of Upper Marlboro, MD and ordained in 2006 by Bishop Mark Anthony Wilson of the Greater Destiny Kingdom Ministries of Baltimore, MD. She was consecrated as Pastor in 2011 by Bishop Ernest C. Dawson of Rehoboth New Life Church Alliance.

Pastor Val is also the CEO of the SIBTT (Sister I've Been There Too) Literary Group, which is a ministry birthed out of the title of the recently released book "Sister, I've Been There Too! But I Came Back to Get You!" (2018) SIBTT is an anthology of testimonies, written by nine vastly different women and one man, about just how good God really is! Pastor Val was a contributing author of, 'A Drink from the Well: Refreshment for the Soul – A Devotional for Women (2008, Amazon), and is currently working on several of her own works for publication soon. In addition to her other written accomplishments, Pastor Val, as an avid encourager, also uses her Facebook page to encourage, inspire, and share the Word of God and her journey daily.

Pastor Valerie is the Director of Pastoral Counseling, and Prayer for I AM My Sister's Keeper. In addition to that, Pastor Val serves on the Board of Directors of several non-profit organizations and ministries birthed and designed to help the Body of Christ heal, be victorious, and overcome life's situations so that the children of God will be made whole, wanting nothing, and thus, allow each of us to go ye therefore and teach, that which Christ taught us!

Pastor Val holds a Bachelor of Science degree in Criminal Justice, with a minor in Corrections, and a Master of Science degree in Public Administration, with a minor in Legal Studies and is employed by the Federal Government.

Favorite scripture: Revelation 12:11 "And they overcame by the blood of the Lamb and the word of their testimony, and they did not love their lives unto death." Pastor Val is married to Robert B. Jones, Jr. and is the mother of two daughters – AlNetta and Jessica.

## CHAPTER 10
## LEARNING TO LOVE THE GIFT – ME!

*Ephesians 3:17-19 (KJV) "That Christ may dwell in your hearts by faith, that ye, being rooted and grounded in love, may be able to comprehend with all saints with a is the breadth and length and depth and height, and to know the love of Christ, which surpasseth knowledge, that ye might be filled with all the fullness of God."*

When I was in junior high school, I entered a speaking contest in which I was introduced to poet Langston Hughes and his poem Mother to Son – "Well son, I'll tell you: Life for me ain't been no crystal stairs. It's had tacks in it, and splinters, and boards torn up, and places with no carpet on the floor – bare. But all the time I'se been a-climbin' on, and rechin' landin's, and turnin; corners, and sometimes goin' in the dark where there ain't been no light. So boy, don't you turn back, Don't you set down on the steps 'cause you finds it's kinder hard. Don't you fall now – For I'se still goin', honey, I'se still climbin', and life for me ain't been no crystal stair." Even today, that poem is framed on my desk to remember that I can't quit! I can't live as "they" think I should! I was built to last, to win, and to conquer everything that this world brings my way!

Growing up in a world which seemed, to me, designed

to destroy me, I did not like myself. I took on the ideals of what my family and those closest to me thought was beautiful, and it wasn't me. I took on their ideas and ideals of what I should have been, what I should wear, the size I should be, the color of my skin, the length of my hair, how I laughed, and even the wideness of my smile. I was an imperfect creature who no one wanted; neither my mother, nor my father and it seemed or appeared to me that the very ones entrusted, who were supposed to love and care for me without borders or limits, didn't want any parts of the real me either.

I spent most of my life feeling useless, unwanted, unloved, and unappreciated. I was tolerated, at best. There were many quiet conversations about me when people thought I was sleeping, calling me all types of names, and making all types of accusations about me that they had no way of proving or knowing, but just spouting, especially if it meant comparing me with someone else, they held very dear. With loud conversations, my mother could have cared less if I heard her, calling me names, and telling people that I would never be good for anything. I felt useless. I couldn't figure out why I was alive, and I thought, like most people who live in a place of constant depression, that everyone would be much better off if I were dead. I got this thought from hearing my mother speak down of me, constantly reminding me that if abortions were legal when she was pregnant with me, I wouldn't be here.

I can remember the first time I decided to take my own life. I was nine years old, and nothing I did seemed to please my mother. I was hiding guilt, blame, and shame about my dad's death. See, I asked to go horseback riding that day and because I was a daddy's girl, we went riding and that was the last day I saw him alive. The guilt, hurt, loneliness, and what seemed to my child's mind as hate from my mother was more than I could handle. I was the fat kid in the family, and as my birth father pointed out, the only "bald-headed girl in the family"; I didn't, in my estimations, look like anyone in my family or resemble anyone at all. I even convinced myself at one point that I was adopted, but I wasn't.

I went upstairs to my bathroom that I shared with my sister and grandfather, filled the tub with water, and got in as if I were taking a bath. Then I slid down under the water. The funny thing was, I couldn't do it. My oldest brother and I were the only ones in the house who could swim, and because of that, I could hold my breath for a long time. But once that time (holding my breath) had gone by, I just couldn't seem to make myself stay under the water, and I would come jumping up gasping for air. I couldn't even die right! I felt like this was an additional failure; I couldn't even succeed in killing myself.

## LEARNING TO LOVE THE GIFT – ME!

The years went on and when I was eleven, my mother put me into foster care. Although the living arrangements improved from the uncertainty of my mother's household, the feelings of not being seen, heard, or considered continued. I even tried to kill myself a few times during both junior high and high school, but of course it didn't work. God had another plan for me.

I pretended to have great self-esteem. Even today when I'm talking to friends that I went to high school with and when I'm honest about where I was emotionally, they find it hard to believe. See, as the "church" we have become masters of disguise. The pain, rejection, abuses, addictions, and all manner of issues that we struggle with, can be waved away, shouted away, or prayed away, just as long as no one knows what's really going on. My generation came to understand that what goes on in our homes, must stay in our home or there would be consequences. But I believe it was actor/producer Tyler Perry who said, "if you keep it in the house, you cannot heal." Well, I didn't heal until many years later.

In 1994, I gave my life to Christ at St. John Freewill Baptist Church, under the leadership of then Pastor Kevin V. Gresham, Sr. I originally gave my life to Christ at the age of 7.5 at Summit Lake Camp, under the leadership of Pastor Bob Crowley, but I had no idea what I was doing then. I just knew I felt something on that mountain, and

I wanted to keep feeling it. But I didn't because life got even more difficult and crazy, especially after my dad died. Then I didn't want anything to do with a god who would allow people to hurt me that way, so I ran from God for years! I was prophesied to while I lived overseas, but I still didn't want to hear anything from God. I was angry, alone, and even though I was married at the time, I still felt unloved.

When I gave my life to God for real this time, with the full understanding of what I was doing, it was different. I had begun to feel a connection with God that I never thought possible. My father in ministry, now Bishop Gresham, supported education and studying the Word of God and although it took me years to even appreciate his approach to teaching, mentoring, and developing leaders, I eventually found my footing with God on my own.

I eventually became a minister of the Gospel, and according to all reports, discussions, etc., I became a powerful preacher and teacher. However, there was one problem, I was doing all of that teaching and preaching feeling that none of God's Word applied to me! I was still living in pain, the memory of the pain, and expectation of more pain. I was still living in the belief that I, somehow, deserved the way people treated me; taking and taking but having nothing to give me in return. I had several breakdowns during this walk with God. I just wanted to tap out, but God wouldn't allow it. Every time I got into a place where I thought I was going to back off and back up from the Gospel, something inside of me wouldn't allow it this time. Something inside of me kept pulling me closer and closer to a loving and merciful God. But that was just the spiritual side; the physical side of me was a mess. Every year I was gaining more and more weight. My relationships never seemed to bare good fruit, no matter what I did, sought, tried, thought, or asked. I was still struggling in every sense of the word.

I never stopped studying the Word of God. I never stopped trying to communicate with God in prayer, and I kept trying to allow the Spirit of God to show me who I needed to glean from, who I needed to be around, and see who my other piece of iron (iron sharpens iron, the Word of God says) so that I can be sharpened. It was difficult, depressing, and I doubted that God even knew who I was because I was such a horrible sinner. All lies from the pit of hell!

> 2 Timothy 2:15 says, "Study to shew thyself approved unto God, a workman that needeth not to be ashamed, rightly dividing the word of truth."

THIS Scripture right here, this Word right here...my God! Changed my life! Romans 8:28, as a matter of fact the entire Chapter of Romans 8, Jeremiah 29:11, and

Ephesians 3:17-19 helped me to see who God really was and what He really expected for my life! Yeah, the Proverbs 31 woman is the Scripture many of us have heard over and over before, which tells us who/what/how we ought to be, but my question was when and who tells us how to get to be her, especially if we've come through hard hurtful, and hateful challenges to get there? Via God's Word and Him ministering to me, allowed certain sisters in my life, who would not let me go back to that place of pain and darkness; this changed my life!

*Psalm 139:14 says, "I will praise thee, for I am fearfully and wonderfully made: marvelous are thy works; and that my soul knoweth right well."*

I got to know God from my soul and not my emotions! I began to seek, ask, and knock and God began to answer in a way that I never thought possible. I was important because God loved me! I finally discovered that He loved me so much that he predestined me for greatness, notwithstanding what man said, thought, or did to make me believe otherwise. I still couldn't see it clearly, but the fog was lifting on the opinions of men; the negative opinions of everyone from my mother on down, no longer mattered because God demonstrated, through His Word and His actions toward me that He loves me! Through my attempted suicides, addictions, sexual encounters outside of marriage, drinking, smoking, cursing, fighting – He was there through it all and He loves me!! My God!

Now, all that was left was to see me as He saw me.

In 1994, as I was preparing to accept my walk as a minister of the Gospel, I asked God to teach me how to love as He loves. I also told God that I didn't want to love anyone else until HE taught me how to love Him first and foremost, and me! That's just what He did. It's taken some years of peeling this onion, but I'm finally in a place where I can see the beauty of who God created me to be. There is a thin line between the words confidence and conceit, and I have nothing to be conceited about; at the same time, I do have the beauty of God in me that I can see and appreciate.

Today, I have made it my life's work to appreciate the gift that is me. I'm still in a world that is comfortable with trying to make me believe that I am less than the least of these, but I'm no longer the wounded creature who needs man's approval. God is my source; He is my rock and my shield. Everything I need, God is! When I'm down, He is the lifter of my head. When my heart is broken, He is my healer. When I'm disappointed in man, He is my shield and buckler, my banner, my peace, joy, and longsuffering. When I feel unwanted, unloved, and unappreciated, I run to Him the more; God is my love!

I can love me today because God does! I can appreciate the beauty of who I am, my intelligence, passion for God's Word, His will, and His ways; I can embrace who God ordained me to be, which is why I will never be everyone's cup of tea. But today, I can also walk pass the mirror, and instead of trying to figure out how to kill what God created and blessed, I can smile and tell myself "Hello gorgeous!"

Listen, I know it might seem like everything and everyone disagrees with who you know you are. I know the world says things like "family is everything!" but you look around and family seems to be finding reasons to cut you off, move away from you, or at least manipulate you into being and doing what benefits them. THAT IS NOT GOD'S PLAN FOR YOUR LIFE, BELOVED! God has greater in store for you, but YOU must look for it! You must seek Him first. You must know that you're worthy of His love! You've got to know that you were not a mistake and that those who say you are, or might imply that you are, or even try to convince you that you are a mistake —nine times out of ten have some healing of their own they refuse to see or do because it's just easier to pick at you than to work on themselves.

God loves you! It doesn't matter who your mother is/was or who your father is/was, what you've done wrong or how you lived your life- God loves you! John 3:16: "For

## LEARNING TO LOVE THE GIFT – ME!

God so loved the world, that He gave His only begotten Son, that whosoever believeth in Him, should not perish, but have everlasting life." and Romans 5:8 "But God commendeth His love toward us, in that, while we were yet sinners, Christ died for us." God has proven His love for you, now it's time for you to learn to love you! You, yes you are a gift to the Body of Christ! No, your name may not be a household brand, or no, your name is not up in lights, but you are just as important to the totality of what God is doing here in the earth, as those who are. You are no insignificant speck that needs to be blotted out, washed out, or kicked out! You, Beloved, are a wonderful, shining example of God's love, and please know, that the power of His presence rests within you.

God's love is enough to release you and bring you over from that dark place, where trying to keep up with the Joneses' is wearing you thin. God's love is enough should you decide to go back to school, start that business, or marry and have a family after your career has taken off! God's love is enough to show you the footsteps in the sand. So, seek Him, God, and learn how to love you, yourself as His gift to the world, today, tomorrow, and the rest of your life.

The day you decide that God is your Father and everything you need, no matter what comes, who leaves, or what they (whoever they are) say. Know and remember for always, that You, as the gift from God you are, that you will begin to shine in a way that will blind your enemies and illuminate the power, purpose, and endless possibilities of who you are in Him. You are a gift, in fact you are a special gift, and He addeth no sorrow to you, and after today, neither will you.

Praise Jesus!

# MOURNING TO MORNING

Reverend Shawnta Moody
Speaker, Entrepreneur, Minister
Owner of Uniquely You Designs, LLC.,
Assistant Vice President, Financial Institution in
Washington, D.C.

## ABOUT THE AUTHOR

Reverend Shawnta Moody is a Speaker, Entrepreneur, Minister and Creative Designer and Owner of Uniquely You Designs, LLC.

Shawnta committed her life to the Lord in 1996 and joined Cornerstone Peaceful Bible Baptist Church (CPBBC), Upper Marlboro, MD, in April 1998. She accepted her call to public ministry in January 2009 and was licensed to preach the gospel on September 21, 2012.

Shawnta currently serves with the Generation Transformed (GT Crew) Youth Ministry and she is an active member of the Intercessory Prayer Ministry, Women of Rare Distinction (W.O.R.D) Ministry and various other ministries at CPBBC.

Shawnta has over 22 years of banking/finance experience and she is an Assistant Vice President with a Financial Institution in Washington D.C. She is currently pursuing her B.S in Psychology.

Reverend. Shawnta is married to Rev. Marcus Moody and is the bonus mom to two young adults.

# Chapter 11
## Mourning to Morning

*"...weeping may endure for a night but JOY comes in the morning." – Psalm 30:5*

Immediately after arriving at the hospital via ambulance, I was whisked away for a sonogram to confirm if I had indeed suffered a miscarriage. As the sonographer began to rub the cold gel across my stomach, I started thinking about the last time I had a sonogram and how the process went. During that appointment, we learned the sex of our baby and listened excitedly and with great expectancy to his heartbeat.

C.J. was to be the first child for both me and his dad so we were overjoyed to go through this new experience together. As we listened to his heartbeat, he was giving us a little show on the monitor. Though his dad and I weren't married and were living in different states, I was able to FaceTime him during appointments, so he didn't miss out on anything.

But this time was different. The sonographer in the Emergency Room asked that I refrain from using FaceTime until she completed the task at hand. She squirted the gel onto my stomach and rubbed the wand around my belly and then up and down she went. It seemed as if hours went by while I was lying there... listening... waiting to see if my worst fear would come to pass. Then suddenly, I heard it! His heartbeat! My "tadpole", as I affectionately called him, was still in there. I exhaled and was so excited. As soon as she heard it, she smiled just a bit but then just as quickly displayed a perplexed look. She then told me that she would need to also perform a transvaginal sonogram. Once done, she was just about to go and get the doctor, but she said something to me, before stepping out, that I will never forget. She looked at me and said, "None of this is your fault."

As she got up, I saw tears in her eyes. Upon her return with the emergency room doctor in tow, they both looked at me, and the doctor told me that my amniotic sac had ruptured and that the baby would be coming sooner than later. I was then wheeled into an Operating Room.

Fully expecting to be released shortly after the procedure, and my not understanding what was happening, I patiently waited in the room and talked to my little tadpole. I prematurely called my friends and family and told them the news. After about an hour or so, I called for a nurse and asked when I would be released. It was then that the severity of the situation was explained to me. The doctor was expecting me to give birth any day now but since the baby was not quite 24 weeks, there was no expectancy that he would survive. I was being kept at the hospital until delivery.

Monday, May 29th, 2006, was Labor Day (both on the calendar and as well for me), while lying in my hospital bed, the doctor came in that morning. He performed a few more tests and told me it would not be much longer. It was a holiday weekend and my OBGYN doctor was out of town, so I found myself at the mercy of a doctor who I didn't know and in a hospital that was not a part of my delivery/birth plan process. After repeating to me again that my child's chance of survival was minimal, the doctor suggested a spontaneous abortion. I declined the abortion and asked the doctor to do whatever he could do to save my baby boy's life, even if it meant I would lose mine. He shook his head as he walked out of my room. A few hours later, my tadpole prepared to make his entry into the world without assistance... and so, out he came. I couldn't get myself to hold him, which is something to this day that I regret. I had the doctor hand him to my mom. She tilted him up so I could see him, and she prayed over him, and he passed away in her (my mom's) arms. He was so little, with tiny hands and tiny feet. He had skinny arms and legs and his skin was the most beautiful dark chocolate color.

After a few extra days in the hospital due to post-delivery complications, I was discharged. My mom took me home and offered to sit with me for a bit, but I declined and told her I wanted to take a nap. So, she headed home. I sat on the couch for a few minutes and then headed to my bedroom. As I approached the door, that's when I saw it...his baby book was on the bed with previous sonograms and other photos laid about. I had forgotten that the last time I was home I was working on putting together his book. That was all it took for me to break. I hadn't shed a tear up until this moment. I hit the floor like a ton of bricks and cried uncontrollably for what seemed like hours. Then I got up, picked up his book and laid across my bed. I looked at each photo and was instantly taken back to the moment the photo was captured and the emotions I felt during those special moments. The happiness. The excitement. The anticipation. It was during these frequent moments of remembering that disappointment began to set in. I thought about all the things that would never happen with this specific child. All the dreams, all the plans, his growing up... all gone... over!

Over the next few days & weeks, I received numerous calls, texts, and visitors. Each time I worked diligently to assure them that I was okay; I smiled during phone conversations & laughed when we, my family and friends were together. But at night behind closed doors I would stare at his baby book and replay all the events over in my head. Did I do something wrong? Did he suffer? Was he scared? Was this God's way of punishing me for having premarital sex? I felt alone, guilty, and angry. Why would God allow me to get pregnant just to have it end like this? I was in a place that I'd never been before... carrying tons of emotions that I couldn't shake. I wanted my baby. I wanted to hold him, and I was angry at God for letting this happen. It wasn't just that I couldn't pray, I didn't want to pray. My heart was broken and no one or nothing could make it better. I was ready to give up. I even told God that since He took my baby, He could come and take me too. I didn't want to be here, on this earth, without him. Each day I waited for God to take my life. I became reckless. I drove without a seatbelt, I crossed streets without looking both ways and I even asked God to take me in my sleep.

This went on for months, the hurts, many types of pain, the disappointments!

I had shut everyone out...even God!!

After about six months of this roller coaster of emotions, something changed. I heard God call my name in the middle of the night and I answered Him, this time. After months of ignoring Him, I finally answered. He told me that He loved me and asked me if I would give Him my heart –with all the broken pieces. I didn't know what to say. I was surprised and shocked that He still cared enough to talk to me, to reach out to me, to call out to me. After all the times I ignored Him, He still pursued me. The Yes left my lips like a whisper and I literally felt His arms wrap around me in comfort and I cried. But this cry was different. Every other time my crying had been desperate but this time, this was a cry of release, relief, if you will. I was releasing the pent-up emotions. I was releasing the burden, the hurt, the pain. Also, I was releasing the frustration and despair. I was letting go of it all to the only One who was strong enough to carry the load for me. The only One who could do something about it. I ran to Him and fell into His hands once again and He held me ever so close. I, respectfully, told God how I felt, how my heart was hurting so, but of course He knew all of this already. I gave Him my doubts, my fears and all the hurts, and right-a-way, the pain just seemed to roll off. I could truly feel His comfort saturate me entirely. My heart didn't seem so heavy anymore. I fell asleep that night and slept like I hadn't slept in such a long time. My sleep was peaceful. I felt His Presence the entire night. The next day, I asked Him why He took my son. It was then that He said something that has stuck with me, even to this day. He told me that there was nothing that He could say that would make me understand it at that time but that He needed me to trust Him. He reminded me how He had been with me each day before the pregnancy, during the pregnancy and after the pregnancy. How He kept a close watch over me, even when I was ignoring Him. He showed me how my post pregnancy complications could've resulted in my death, but He had kept me. He brought back to my remembrance all the actions I had taken after CJ's death that should've led to my death as well. Day by day I began to reconnect with God. I didn't hide my feelings from Him. I promised Him all my heart and that's what I gave Him. All the ugliness, messiness... all of it. I held none of it back. And as we met daily, He began to heal my heart. He began to change my heart. I no longer felt the pangs of sorrow over the loss of CJ. I no longer envied those that had babies after me or felt that somehow my not having CJ meant there was something wrong with me. He released me from the guilt I was experiencing and holding on to. I was coming into a place where I was able to speak openly about CJ and not start crying.

It was in that moment, in that deep valley of my life, that I realized that's when my relationship with God shifted. It went beyond the surface. It went beyond religion. He wasn't just the God I read about in the Bible or the One that I listened to sermons about Sunday after Sunday. It became personal. It was there where I learned that in my weaknesses, His strength is indeed made perfect. I was not alone and that God, the One who created the world, cared about Shawnta Kianna.

I've come to learn that in times of loss, yes it changes us, but it doesn't have to define us, and we don't have to grieve for the rest of our lives. We may go through dark moments, but they don't have to last forever. Weeping may endure for the night, but JOY will come in the morning!

God is faithful, and regardless of the loss He can heal our hearts if we will just give Him the broken pieces. Readers, I warmly, respectfully share with you to open up to Him and let Him take you from Mourning to Morning. 😊

# FINDING LOVE AGAIN BY STARTING WITHIN

Christal Spence Newkirk
Bestselling Author, Business Coach, HR Consultant
CEO of AboveHR Solutions, LLC
www.ChristalNewkirk.com

## ABOUT THE AUTHOR

Christal Spence Newkirk is a Bestselling Author, Business Coach and HR Consultant with over 20 years of Diversity Recruitment, Corporate Talent Acquisition and Affirmative Action Planning experience, working with Fortune 500 companies such as Siemens, The Home Depot, AT&T, The Coca-Cola, Goodyear, and Honeywell. She earned her Master of Science Management Degree in Process Improvement and A Bachelor's Degree of Marketing from North Carolina State University.

In Christal's free time, she loves volunteering with SCORE as their VP HR & Certified Business Mentor. SCORE, a national nonprofit, provides free business mentoring, education and resources to entrepreneurs who are interested in launching or growing their businesses.

Christal and her husband, Rodney, currently manage a Real Estate Investment Firm and a HR Consulting & Coaching Firm. They reside in Fort Mill, SC with their fur baby, Dundee and love traveling with family and friends.

Visit www.ChristalNewkirk.com to download your free copy of Healing Affirmations ebook.

# CHAPTER 12
# FINDING LOVE AGAIN BY STARTING WITHIN

"I'm tired of being alone. I'm tired of waiting for Mr. Right to find me. I'm tired of failed relationship after failed relationship. I thought I would be married by now with kids and a beautiful home. "Dating is hard after divorce, so how much longer, Lord?"

Do these statements resonate with you? These thoughts were always running through my head. It took a decade after my divorce until I met my Mr. Right. Over those years, the battle of my mind and emotions were constant until I discovered the healing path that would lead me on my self-love, growth journey.

My low self-esteem issues began in childhood. While growing up, I did not have a relationship with my father. I knew his name but never met him in-person until age sixteen. This created an emotional void in my life. At a young age, I remember longing for a father I never had. There were many times when I just needed a loving embrace from my father's arms, but he was never there emotionally or physically. I felt abandoned when he remarried, adopted kids, and started a new life without me. He never called or visited for my birthdays or holidays.

My lack of self-love led to becoming a people pleaser and I made bad choices concerning male relationships. I gave too much time to others and rarely thought of my needs in dating relationships. Self-love was foreign concept for me as a young adult. I dated men that were cheaters, liars and had commitment phobia. Growing up, I was blind to all the beautiful ways Father God had uniquely designed and created me. I did not see my beauty when I looked in the mirror.

During my junior year in college, I met my ex-husband and dated him for two years. We were good friends and enjoyed spending time together, but I was not in love. I'm not sure at twenty-one I knew what love was. Graduating from grad school with honors was a big accomplishment for me at twenty-five. Although the degree helped improve my self confidence and opened the door for job opportunities, it did not change my marriage. The end of my marriage was a painful experience, and the divorce process took me on an emotional roller coaster ride for two years. My transformational experience started New Year's Eve 1999. My divorce had been final for seven months, and I felt disconnected mentally and emotionally. I was ready for change! While attending a New Year's Eve service with friends, I rededicated my life to Jesus Christ and joined a new church. This decision started my self-love and emotional healing journey.

When I rededicated my life to Christ, I embraced my new spiritual relationships, wholeheartedly and changed my lifestyle including my toxic friendship circle. As I began to study the Bible and attend church regularly, I identified my root issues and I understood how rejection and abandonment molded my emotional life. As you know, we act within the context of how we think and what we believe about ourselves from childhood. So, one of my first steps on my spiritual- growth journey was creating positive self-talks based upon God's Word. Why? Because I now believe that I am who God says I am. Through years of counseling, studying God's Word and developing a new mindset, I successfully worked through the wounds in my heart; I've grown and developed in self-love and,su I've embraced a positive self confidence. Ten years after rededicating my life to Jesus Christ, I met my husband, Rodney Newkirk.

During Labor Day weekend 2009, my mom and her close friend, Mrs. Ruth, introduced us virtually and gave Rodney my phone number. At that time, I lived in Houston and Rodney lived in Las Vegas. On our first conversation, we talked on the phone for two hours. I felt an unusual connection shortly thereafter. It wasn't like anything I had experienced before. Rodney's words touched the innermost part of my heart. We instantly connected spiritually as we shared our faith, testimonies, and our past victories during our many talks. After a week of conversing, I wanted to explore further and get to know him. We talked on the phone for the next thirty days without sending each other pictures, because we desired something different. We wanted to connect spiritually and emotionally during our FaceTime, or Skype conversations. This was very important to us, since we both had been married before; we wanted to do this without physical or sexual distractions.

About three weeks into our conversations, Rodney said, "The Holy Spirit revealed to me that you are a Proverbs 31 woman."

After 30 days, we finally met in person as Rodney was completing a project in Baton Rouge, Louisiana, and as I mentioned earlier, I was living in Houston at that time. After our first meeting, Rodney asked, "Is it okay if I commit to get to know you exclusively?" I excitedly said, "Yes!" While dating, the Holy Spirit revealed certain battles we would face with those close to us, and we needed to protect our marriage. Our greatest battle to date has been with those in our very close circle. After six months of dating, Rodney and I exchanged wedding vows...without family and friends present. With much prayer, we decided not to share our wedding day with anyone until we were ready. Some family members and friends were not informed until one year later. Our decision was intentional, and we trusted God's instructions.

Our marriage has been very challenging at times, but we understood our assignment when we said "Yes" and accepted our purpose-driven covenant. We also embraced the process to receive God's promises as He prepares us for the next level in our marriage. Let's be clear. A purpose-driven marriage is not easy. I believe that for us to grow to the next level, we must successfully pass the test at our current level. As we graduate to the next level, the lessons are more difficult.

There are no short-cuts to a successful, purpose driven marriage. If you are unfamiliar with the term "purpose-driven life," I highly recommend Rick Warren's book titled "The Purpose Driven Life" as your next selection. Rodney and I will celebrate twelve years of marriage on March 12, 2022. As expected, our decision to marry has been the best investment of our lives.

Prior to meeting Rodney, I prayed Ephesians 1:17-18 over my future husband for almost 10 years. "How did you know that Rodney was your husband? Was there a sign from God? Did God specifically tell you that Rodney was your husband? These were a few questions people asked when I shared our love story. Here are my non-negotiables that I established on my spiritual-growth journey, prior to meeting Rodney.

## 1. *Know your unique design*

Since my divorce, I also realized that I did not know the characteristics of the uniquely designed wife, specifically as to what type of man I was created to share my life with. According to Ephesians 2:10, I am uniquely designed by Father God to do good works on a right path and enjoy the good life that He already made ready for me. I believed that my husband and I were called to do this "good work" together. Therefore, my unique design is rare. I believe I was created to fit and support a certain type of man based upon my personality, purpose, etc. Once I understood and accepted this truth, my dating life changed. I studied different types of personality assessments to understand my strengths, gifts, and talents so that I would make better relationship choices. I started dating men differently based upon my new self-identity, my new-found spiritual relationship with God and my specific purpose in life. As I developed in self-love and self confidence, I attracted the unconditional love I desired in my godly marriage; I no longer tolerated certain behaviors from any man that claimed he loved me.

## 2. *Create your non-negotiables' list*

After my divorce, I created my non-negotiable list

through prayer, wise counsel, education, past experiences, and self-assessments. As a HR Consultant, I work closely with my consulting clients to hire candidates for a specific job. Each position has a job description with key responsibilities, required skills and preferred skills. I used this same concept during my dating process. My non-negotiables were my job requirements for my husband. I believed that my marriage was purposefully driven. Therefore, we are responsible for doing "good works according to Ephesians 2:10. So, I was very intentional in my dating process. I also believed in a 90-day probationary period just like a Fortune 500 company. During this probationary period, I made sure I did not fall in love with the ideal of marriage, however, I did evaluate Rodney's behaviors as they related to my list. My four non-negotiables (job requirements) included:

a. **Spiritual intimacy** – someone who is already married to Jesus Christ, a tither and he believed in praying in the Holy Spirit with the evidence of tongues.

b. **Entrepreneurial spirit** – someone who wanted more than a job, had a strong business acumen, and had the work ethic to build a business as he acquired skills from the day job.

c. **Purpose alignment** – someone who was already walking in their purpose. One key question in my dating process was "Do our purposes align?"

**d. Physical** – someone who took care of his body with proper exercising and nutrition, and we must have a mutual attraction.

*3. The tribe of wise couples*

While Rodney and I dated, our biggest challenge was communication and conflict resolution. Rodney and I have different personalities and we handle conflicts accordingly. However, we desired to learn how to communicate properly during the conflicts. We have three couples in our close circle who played an important role in our marriage. I've personally watched these three marriages closely as a single woman and both Rodney and I learned a lot from each couple while dating. We are forever thankful for my twin Chris and my close friend/sister-in-law Kristy, my sister/close friend Angel and her husband Courtney and my close friend, Tasha, and her husband Darien Sykes for being our marriage mentors and role models over the years. Remember, wisdom comes from a relationship with Jesus Christ. Please make sure you surround your relationship with successful couples who are praying for you and want to share their battles, victories, and wisdom with you.

*4. Follow after peace*

At the end of the day, let peace be your guide. One of my favorite peace scriptures is "Let the peace of Christ [the inner calm of one who walks daily with Him] be the controlling factor in your heart [deciding and settling questions that arise]. To this peace indeed you were called as members in one body [of believers]. And be thankful [to God always]." (Colossians 3:15 AMP) As you give your relationship time and continue to seek God, truth will be revealed. Father God loves you and He wants the best for you, but you must continue to seek and follow peace.

On my self-love growth journey, I've also learned to develop healthy boundaries for all relationships, especially those in my inner circle and potential business opportunities. "A prudent person sees trouble coming and ducks; a simpleton walks in blindly and is clobbered." (Proverbs 22:3 Message)

Several years ago, my husband shared this scripture with me while I was going through a challenging time with close relationships. I took a break from the relationships and spent time studying God's Word, embracing emotional healing, and developing healthy boundaries. When the relationships were reconciled, I was stronger emotionally and crystal clear on what healthy boundaries look like personally. Now, I understand that wisdom only comes from Jesus Christ. Therefore, I intentionally invite God into every relationship by asking Him to reveal the true intent of an individual's heart, what His purpose is in the relationship, and any hidden agendas according to

Ephesian 1:17-18. Once I've received direction and clarity for the relationship, I quickly remove myself from any possible toxicity and drama with no questions asked. My goal is to intentionally align with God's purpose for my life. This new behavior has helped me to put people in the right place in my heart and decrease drama, disappointments and hurt feelings due to wrong expectations. My prayer is that this chapter inspires you to win within through loving yourself first, creating non-negotiables relationships and setting healthy boundaries in every relationship.

# GRACEFULLY BROKEN: LOOKING BACK TO MOVE FORWARD

LuDrean Howard-Peterson
Strategist, Coach
CEO, Delivering On Ideas & Thoughts (DOIT)
Founder, DO IT Empowers, Inc.
Host of "Let's Do It" Talk Show

## ABOUT THE AUTHOR

LuDrean Howard-Peterson is the CEO of Delivering On Ideas & Thoughts (DOIT) and Founder of DO IT Empowers, Inc. As a Career/Business Strategist and a Certified Christian Life Coach, she specializes in turning DREAMERS into DOERS.

LuDrean is extremely enthusiastic about helping others optimize ideas and achieve their personal and professional goals. This HR Guru has been in this industry for 30 years and is highly sought after for resume-writing, interview preparation, career changes and unbiased coaching. She has a proven record of achieving groundbreaking success in the U.S and across the globe (China, India, South Africa, Latin America, Europe, and Mexico).

LuDrean is the Host of "Let's Do It" Talk Show; #1 Bestselling Visionary Author; as well as an international speaker and international emcee.

She holds dual master's degrees: an MBA and Master of Science in Management (MSM), with an emphasis in Human Resources Management, as well as a Master Project Management Certification.

# Chapter 13
# Gracefully Broken: Looking Back to Move Forward

## *GRACEFULLY BROKEN*

*Is it possible for you to be fixed by the very thing that has broken you?*

### Gracefully...

For most of my life, I have struggled with severe anxiety when triggered by the loss and illness of family and friends. This is something I have openly shared with many. During the encountered episodes, my ability to focus or think would come to a halt. It consisted of sleepless nights, looking at the ceiling and praying to see the daylight. It was My Mommy who would console and pray for me, however when she transitioned November 2020, I felt lost and wondered who would console, pray with, and love me the way she did. Seconds after receiving this horrific news, the Holy Ghost spoke and comforted me, which provided my answer...God will.

The day before My Sister and I could bury our mother, I received news that My Sister was terminally ill and there wasn't anything else that the doctors could do to help. Hospice was their recommendation. She transitioned

February 2021. Who would help me to get through this traumatic experience? The answer remained the same...God will.

In the darkest season ever experienced in my life, my sacrificial offering was my faith and trust in God. Was I triggered by the loss? Yes, but this time it was different. Was I broken? Absolutely! I was broken, but gracefully broken.

> *"For by grace are ye saved through faith; and that not of yourselves: it is the gift of God,"* (Ephesians 2:8, KJV).

## BROKEN...

The events of the past year have changed my life forever and positioned me into a posture of constant reflection. My history with anxiety, relative to hospitals and deaths, goes back as early as a toddler. I suffered with chronic asthma and spent most winter months very ill. During grade school, the recurring episodes of struggling to breathe and being rushed to the hospital often left me thinking that I was going to die. The next major trauma was when I was in the third grade.

My classmate, Frankie, collapsed during recess and transitioned. The losses and incidents became a recurring theme, totaling hundreds and far too numerous to name. The most concise way to share the depth of my brokenness is by detailing the 19 days of experiencing the deepest heartbreak and darkest period of my lifetime.

September 2020, I had a dream My Mommy transitioned. I began to have deep conversations with her, based on the dream, but couldn't have imagined her passing within two months. The next 19 days of my life would become a real-life rollercoaster, filled with sudden drops, twists, and turns, raging with a rapid speed and powered with a powerful force. Buckle up your seat belt and grab some tissue.

Here we go:

November 17, 2020 – My Mommy transitioned.

November 30, 2020 – The reminders to take My Mommy to her doctor appointment and to meet My Sister at the funeral home to view Mom's body popped up on my phone at the same time. I answered the phone to a sobbing cry from My Sister, struggling to tell me the heartbreaking news that her doctors would not release her from the hospital to attend our Mommy's viewing and funeral. The next voice I heard in her background was the doctor saying, "there isn't anything else that we can do for you…we recommend hospice." Huh?

December 1, 2020 – I laid My Mommy to rest, while My Sister viewed via live stream.

December 6, 2020 – I celebrated My Mommy's First Heavenly Birthday with a gravesite balloon release, surrounded by immediate family.

Wow! I am still in disbelief of how my world was suddenly and forever changed.

## *LOOKING BACK TO MOVE FORWARD*

Is looking back helpful or hurtful to you? I could debate both sides of this argument.

### LOOKING BACK...

Neel Raman (Inspiring Greatness) wrote, "If things from the past aren't addressed and remain incomplete, they can feel like an anchor and slow you down as you make changes in your life."

As a child in grade school, I was traumatized from thinking I was going to die every time I struggled to breathe or was rushed to the hospital. As a witness, I saw the transition of a classmate as we played during recess further inflicted trauma. These wounds were not healed yet and they kept resurfacing each time I experienced the death and illness of a loved one. It wasn't until I began seeing a therapist that I really focused on doing the work to address the root issue. It required me to look back, which was the only way I could heal.

## To Move Forward

Next, a quote from Michael McMillian, "You can't start the next chapter of your life if you keep re-reading the last one" sparked my attention. There is a definitive truth to this statement. You simply cannot occupy space in the past and the present at the same time. In this case, we are advised not to look back because it can cause us to get stuck. There is the possibility that looking back could pave a pathway to relapsing back to that very place of hurt, doubt, or destruction from which you worked so hard to escape.

Lastly, T.B. Joshua wrote, "Avoid the trap of looking back unless it is to glorify God for what He has done." This quote sums up my thoughts. The global coronavirus (COVID-19) pandemic wreaked havoc and caused the world to shut down for the majority of 2020 which left behind remnants that will forever change how we live. For me, the year, specifically the 17th of November, will forever represent the beginning of the darkest season I've ever experienced. My emotions were all over the place which included me spending countless hours pondering over the trials I faced. It was in the "looking back" that I was reminded of all that God had already done for me. I was able to find peace and comfort in knowing that God was able to and would continue to comfort me throughout.

For these reasons, I strongly encourage you to take moments to intentionally look back to ensure there isn't anything unhealed preventing your growth and to see from whence God has brought you as encouragement. The key word is "look"; look back, but don't turn back around. Look back to help you move forward. Reflecting on the past can remind us of how far we have come, and it serves as an encouragement to inspire us to persevere. For me, it sprinkles reminders and memories of gratitude that help me to reminisce about God's grace!

## ALL ROADS LEAD TO GOD

In closing, I realized that facing my anxiety helped me to overcome my anxiety. It was in my looking back to understand the root of my issue, where I was able to" fix" my problem.

My beloved mother and my dear sister, both transitioned exactly 19 days prior to their birthdays. Patterns, sequences, and timings of events stood out to me and left me more stunned. On top of this, on the 4th of February, during a routine medical examination, I asked my gynecologist to check out a change in an existing noncancerous lump in my breast. My doctor was very concerned and requested that I have a mammogram and ultrasound, immediately. The results were unfavorable.

After several medical examinations and a series of

medical procedures, surgery was recommended. It would require me to be tested and quarantined between each visit. During this time, my routine was driving an hour each way to Johns Hopkins Hospital every other day to spend the night with my sister. I didn't have the capacity to worry about me. Immediately, I totally surrendered the situation to God and prayed for guidance. I continued to be by My Sister's bedside, and I postponed the procedures and surgery. My testimony is full of God's grace, goodness, and guidance. God gets all the glory!

God's Grace. The Trial and Triumph. Even when you interfere with God's plan or try to be in control, God will help you to get back on the right path…either by force or by choice. When an assignment seems too tough for us to manage, we see it as a trial. Sometimes we are placed in situations where there aren't any options other than to trust and depend on God. This was me when I first stepped foot in My Sister's hospital room. God orchestrated the situation. I thought I was being escorted to the business office to accompany my niece regarding medical affairs. Due to my anxiety, I would not have voluntarily visited My Sister.

When she was first diagnosed with cancer, I rarely visited her in the hospital. I couldn't stomach it. So here we are, five years later and God had a different plan for this round. Once I stepped into her room, it was the point of no return. When leaving, I asked how did we get to visit her when no visitors were allowed due to COVID-19? I learned that the name of the visit was "End of Life Visit." I got to my car and cried; the name alone was heartbreaking. As I was sobbing in the car, a few earthly angels sent me "right on time" messages via texts. They were just what I needed to pull myself together to face the hour-long drive home. God's comfort on that one day gave me just enough comfort to returning again, and again, and again.

My Sister's death was traumatizing. Towards the end on each day thereafter, I saw her increasingly deteriorate. The night before she transitioned, her distinguished features started to diminish. At this point the visits became unbearable, but I know God comforted and helped me get through them. Not only did He help me to conquer my years of unease with hospital visits, but more importantly, my visits with her allowed me to honor My Sister's wish...which was not to die alone. I, along with her son, was at her bedside as she took her last breath. I know that I did not have the capability or strength to complete that assignment on my own. God grants us unmerited favor to get us through the trials and the assignments that He predestined for our lives.

## God's Goodness. The Trial and Triumph.

Within 19 days of burial, we celebrated her first Heavenly Birthday with a balloon release. I left the gravesite and headed to the first of what would begin a series of medical appointments. There was no time to grieve. Life was throwing me blow after blow. So, my next trial was that my doctors thought I had cancer. Over the next few months, I had twenty medical appointments. Each visit appeared less promising than the ones before, and eventually, I had a breast lumpectomy on April 23rd. The results were negative/noncancerous! Thank You God!

As I was adding post-surgery appointments to my calendar, I was reminded that both My Mommy and My Sister transitioned 19 days prior to their birthdays. With my birthday (June 4th) approaching, it led me to count back 19 days from it. I marked May 15th on my calendar. This also happened to be the day our family was scheduled for a flight to Florida for our vacation. Anxiety began to creep in with "what if's" questions. What if I die on the flight to Florida? What if my daughter and her family died too? And then the Holy Spirit whispered in my ear, "What if I continued to comfort you"? God is a comforter!

Early on My Mommy was my traveling partner. We took at least two trips a year, a road trip and then somewhere special for her birthday. Recently while on a vacation to

Massanutten, I was out on a walk, and out of routine and habit, I begin to think to myself "What are me and Mommy going to do today?" It hit me hard realizing that she wasn't at the vacation house waiting for me to return from my morning walk. Oh, how the precious memories made me smile and laugh. To the extent that they overshadowed the grief.

*"Surely goodness and mercy shall follow me all the days of my life...," (Psalms 23:6, KJV).*

God's Guidance. Tribulations and Training. "Count it All Joy!" It took me 50 years to truly understand this verse, especially relating to grief. I couldn't understand why funerals and hospitals were unbearable for me. It was even more perplexed because of the substantial number of family members and friends who transitioned over the past three years. If funerals were so hard, then why did God keep sending me to them. How was I to count the pain from attending so many funerals all joy? Now, I see that each one was a steppingstone, serving as preparation to prepare me for what was to come. Trust God even when you can't face Him.

God's Glory. The Test and Testimony. Losing My Mommy and My Sister, two extremely close family members in such a close period of time, has been by far the most traumatic event that I have ever experienced.

My history of anxiety triggered by death and ill loved ones is openly known to those who are close to me. Because of past experiences, I could not have imagined experiencing the magnitude to which God is comforting me. Overcoming such an intense degree of anxiety, especially during my darkest season of mourning and heartbreak has been unexplainable. This is nothing short of a modern-day miracle for me and for those who have witnessed God's peace and covering over me.

God created us for His glory and instructs us to do everything for His Glory. In all that we do, we are to recognize and acknowledge that everything that we do, should be done for God's glory.

This year was full of firsts without My Mommy and My Sister. The one-year mark of My Mommy's transition caused butterflies. In preparation, I took off the entire week from my job. The night before my heart ached so bad. I remember praying to God asking Him to comfort me. He did. I honored My Mommy, Martha, by volunteering at Martha's Table, a nonprofit organization. I had no idea that the feelings of hurt, and fulfillment could occupy the same space. They can!

> I know that it is only by the grace of God that I am still standing.

To help me through my healing journey, I designed and

published a prompted journal, We All Heal Differently. It's a companion to my recently released book project, We All Grieve Differently (Available at www.do-it-delivers/com/book-projects and on Amazon).

# THANKFUL, GRATEFUL AND BLESSED TO LEND A HELPING HAND

Maria Thorpe
Professional, Speaker, Author
Chess Enthusiast

## ABOUT THE AUTHOR

Maria Thorpe currently works for the Federal Government in the engineering arena. She is also a speaker, mentor, co-author, and real estate agent. She has mentored numerous students and professionals in Science, Technology, Engineering, and Math (STEM). She has spoken at events, including local schools and colleges inspiring young girls and empowering women, about being the best they can be with the gifts and talents that God has given them.

Maria is the co-owner of Waldorf Chess Club Inc., which she founded with her husband. She works with children as young as five years old, helping them find their inner strength, hone, or improve their decision-making skills, and build confidence through the game of chess.

Maria is a graduate of Drexel University, Philadelphia, PA with a Bachelor of Science in Electrical Engineering. She is a graduate of Pennsylvania State University with a Master of Engineering, Engineering Science Degree and she has received numerous awards, accolades and honors.

# CHAPTER 14
## *Thankful, Grateful and Blessed to Lend a Helping Hand*

*"The highest test of the civilization of any race is in its willingness to extend a helping hand to the less fortunate."*
– Booker T. Washington

So often in life we believe we can do everything by ourselves. It is great to be independent and believe in your capabilities, but it does not mean you can't ask for help when you need it. Over the years, I have found that to be the best you can be, you may find that asking for assistance will be the key to your success. Sometimes no matter how hard you try, the solution just won't come to you, and for that reason alone, you may want to collaborate. Additionally, you may want to have some diversity in your solutions, or you may need help because you are on a tight schedule and do not have the time to get to a resolution. Furthermore, you may not have the ability to solve the problem alone and you just need another set of eyes or a pair of hands. Whatever the reason is, having a diverse set of solutions and associates around you may help you find the answers quicker, in many situations.

I have had people in my life who don't know me or my

story, say "your life has been so easy". I would respond "not really". Life is not easy for me or anyone, but life is what you make it. If you think life is hard, it will be and if you think life is easy, it possibly will be. You are what you believe you are. As a young girl growing up, I recall walking down the street in my neighborhood, upset that I had gotten in trouble, yet again, for not getting my hundreds of tasks complete at home. At least it felt like a hundred tasks. My solution was to get up a little earlier on Saturday morning to try and get things started. This way I could get my work done sooner and meet up with friends, socialize and do the activities I enjoyed.

However, before, I could get to the fun part of my day, I had a few more problems to solve and tasks to complete. Not only did I have to complete my chores at my house, but my mother told a neighbor down the street that I could complete some errands for her too. This day had just gotten worse; I felt like my Saturday was simply being wasted on chores and that I would never get to the fun things I had planned with my friends.

Once I had completed most of my weekly chores, I prepared to take a break, however before that I had to go and pick up the dry cleaning. When I returned, to finish my final tasks, I was informed that I was required to go to the neighbor's home because she really needed help. Needless to say, I was not happy at first that I had to spend

## THANKFUL, GRATEFUL AND BLESSED TO LEND A HELPING HAND

my free time helping someone else do their work. But I recall my mom saying be glad you have the health to help someone else, because if you are lucky enough to get to old age, hopefully someone will want to help you!

My mother did not indicate who I would be helping, but to my surprise it was one of the community elders. The elderly neighbor did not have any family that I was aware of, and she was in desperate need of assistance. She was a very lovely person, and she always watched out for the children in the neighborhood. When she saw someone doing something wrong, she would try to correct the behavior they were displaying. She was like the neighborhood grandmother and by the time she was done speaking with you, you would be glad to have had the conversation.

Sometimes when people get a little older, they need extra care, so subsequently, I was glad I could assist her with whatever she needed. She provided me with her list of tasks to be completed; tidy up the kitchen, vacuum the carpet, sweep the floors, and dust where needed.

The list was long for just a couple of hours of work, and I was not sure if I was going to get everything completed. I believed it would take the reminder of my Saturday afternoon. The thought of having to dust, mop and sweep was not my idea of a fun afternoon.

I began the tasks, working as diligently as I could. I was paying attention to details, making sure I did not miss a spot. I wanted everything to be perfect and I wanted to make my mom proud to know she could depend on me to assist others. I started with sweeping the floors then putting away the wash, and finally I started dusting the furniture. I was proud of myself for getting the list completed as quickly as I did. I was finally finished with the last task assigned to me, so I walked over to informed her that I was done. It wasn't as late as I thought it would be and I was happy because I still had time to catch up with my friends and have some fun. Afterwards, I informed her that I was complete with the chores for her. She then began to inspect the work and she smiled as she ran her finger across the furniture, trying to identify if I had missed a spot. Overall, she was pleased with what I had accomplished, but then she said there was one more item she forgot and wanted me to compete. She asked could I dust the curio cabinet. I informed her that I did dust the outside, however she wanted me to dust the inside of the cabinet where she had numerous 'Knick Knacks'. I looked at the task and knew it would take some time to complete.

As I opened the glass door to the cabinet it had the most beautiful objects. Many of the delicate items were made of porcelain and glass. For each item I picked up to dust she shared a story about it and why it held a special place

## THANKFUL, GRATEFUL AND BLESSED TO LEND A HELPING HAND

in her heart and cabinet. I was careful because I was afraid, I would break the objects. However, I was honored that she trusted me with her cherished items. I dusted item after item and when I finally got to the last one, I placed it gently in its special place in the cabinet. She again checked my work and was very pleased. She was happy that her home was clean, dusted and back in order. Not once did she complain about how I did the task she gave me that day nor did she point out what I did incorrect. She was just grateful for my help that day and I was glad I could lend a hand.

I learned a lot from that experience. One thing I learned was how blessed I was at being able to spend the afternoon with someone who had complete confidence in me, trusted me and my ability to get the job done, even though I had no idea what the task was going to entail. I gave it my all because I wanted to do a good job for her. I also learned that things don't always go the way you expect them to go, or you think they should go, but you can always choose how you respond and your attitude towards any given situation.

This became a weekly activity during that summer, and I was glad I was able to assist such a wonderful person who had given so much to the youth in the community. She had a profound influence on my life, and I was thankful I could help one of my mother's dearest friends. She was so grateful that someone took time from their day to come by and help with something that was so important to her. The experience reminded me of the following quote.

> "Those who influenced me the most are not those who pointed out all my faults, but those who knew God was bigger than my shortcomings. Those who influenced me the most didn't just point a finger, they held out a helping hand". – Phil Callaway

As I walked back home, I began to recall the conversation and stories that were shared with me. Remember, when I started the day off, I had planned to hang out with my friends, but I embraced the change that was placed in front of me, which was helping a neighbor with some tasks around her home. Spending time with her really changed my outlook on life. The knowledge I received about friendship, life challenges, honesty, being the best version of myself, and having integrity in all that you do, empowered me to proceed to take action of my dreams for my future, which made me feel powerful. I thought I was there to help her, but in turn she ended up helping me visualize my future.

I would charge you to document or record the last conversation you had with an elderly person that you trust and respect and write down five (5) lessons you learned from that conversation and implement them in

# THANKFUL, GRATEFUL AND BLESSED TO LEND A HELPING HAND

your daily life. I believe it will make all the difference in your growth.

When I returned home, I thanked my mother for allowing me the opportunity to spend the day with her friend. Oftentimes we call on God to fix the situation or help us before we have even tried to do something about the situation ourselves, but sometimes He wants us to think about it and try to learn from it and grow thereby from it. It becomes part of His plan and our life's lesson. I told my friends later that day about the lessons I learned which were invaluable, and I carried this knowledge with me every day.

I share this story with you because I believe that the lessons you learn when you are young may definitely help you to be successful as you go through adulthood, at work and in your personal life, if you just take the time to remember how you felt and the impact it had when you were in a situation similar to the one, I was in. That day with her and subsequently, the other days as well, I learned quite a bit about myself and the ability I have which can bring a smile to someone's life. The assistance and support we give to others can have a tremendous positive impact on us. I had the wonderful opportunity to grow and learn about myself and another human being. That day helped me find my purpose. My purpose was to help people with their dreams and desires. In spending the day with my mother's friend, it helped me to start thinking differently about the impact I can have on someone else's life.

Today, as I reach out to our youth and families, through my speaking engagements, mentoring and the Waldorf Chess Club, I try to instill in them the value and positiveness of that which was both impacted and imparted to me on that day. That is, our neighbors are of significance, and they are important; the elderly have quite a bit of knowledge to share; also, what you think and bring to the discussion is important too. I try to help our youth build confidence in themselves, make plans, be positive and be consistent, intentionally. Remember to always put your best foot forward and do what you say you are going to do. Be true to your word. Respecting and valuing each other is an honor. These characteristics can help you achieve the success you want in life.

*Life is too short not to create, not to love, and not to lend a helping hand to our brothers and sisters. – Eric Maisel*

# EMPOWERED TO WRITE – NOW!

Minister Allison Gregory Daniels
Founder, Allison Daniels' Ministries, LLC
Founder/CEO of the Write 2 Finish Now! Book Program
Founder/CEO of AGD Publishing Company
Founder/CEO of Women Empowered 2 Win
Organization
Monday Morning Facebook Live @ 5am Segment.
Host of two (2) Podcasts – Authors Chat with Allison
and The Authors Lab

## ABOUT THE VISIONARY AUTHOR

Minister Allison Gregory Daniels, an Awarding-Winning, 4x Bestselling Author, has written over 31 books, and as a Life Coach, Allison shares that she has been extremely honored and blessed to help empower women in various stages of their lives who are seeking professional and personal growth through venues that provide motivation, awareness, and mentoring.

Allison teaches life skills to women in the form of discipleship, stewardship and servant leadership via networking, teaching, mentoring, workshops, special events and conferences. She is the owner of Allison Daniels' Ministries, LLC; Founder/CEO of the Write 2 Finish Now! Book Program where she teaches writers how to write their books and share their stories. She is also the Founder/CEO of AGD Publishing Company; it is her mission to turn writers into successful authors, one book at a time. She is the Founder/CEO of Women Empowered 2 Win Organization, which is geared to empowering to educate women of all ages, to lead with authority.

As stated above, that she is an accomplished Author, Speaker, Coach, and Licensed Minister she also has a Monday Morning Facebook Live @ 5am Segment, and she is a former Contributing Co-Host of the WBGR radio show "LetsDoThis". She is the Host of two (2) Podcasts – Authors Chat with Allison and The Authors Lab. She uses her books, coaching and her mentoring skills as tools to help and assist those who are ready to lead with authority, lead with clarity and lead with confidence toward their next level up. Her passionate mission is to motivate and aspire others to dream big and fulfill their God-given destiny.

# CHAPTER 15
## *EMPOWERED TO WRITE – NOW!*

*"And the LORD answered me, and said, Write the vision, and make it plain upon tables, that he may run that readeth it." Habakkuk 2:2*

Yes, you can do this. You are Empowered to WRITE Now!

Maybe God has been nudging you from time to time to write your story, so now is the time. We all have a story down on the inside and now it is time for it to be manifested. I declare that God is birthing something BIG in your life! It's time for you to allow Him to push you forward in birthing your gift; to deliver this gift –the gift He has down on the inside of you. It is time for you to take charge of your life and tell your own story! You have the Write 2 Finish Your Own Story. You have the Write 2 Finish the Ending of your Own Story. Today begins a new day, a new chapter for you to take back your life and begin to live again. It's time for you to eliminate the self-defeated beliefs you have about yourself, and Write it down, now.

You are Empowered to WRITE Now! It's time for you to

birth your assignment and write, share, and publish your own story. Every day we learn several things we must do to move forward and a few of those things consists of loving, sharing, forgiving, and moving on and learn how to accept yourself and enjoy your journey.

You are Empowered to WRITE Now! Each day we must begin to write our own chapter and turn the pages from one chapter of our lives to the next chapter. Say, did you know that writing down your own story is a healing process? Yes, it is, so we must begin to embrace who we are and take control of our emotions; we must cease from that inferior feeling to others and move forward with our lives.

> "And the LORD answered me, and said, Write the vision, and make it plain upon tables, that he may run that readeth it." Habakkuk 2:2

You are Empowered to WRITE Now! The Word of God says *Where there is no vision, the people perish: but he that keepeth the law, happy is he.* Do you have a vision to see your book written, to have your story told and to take back your voice and your life?

What is the definition of **VISION!** A vision is something seen in a dream, trance, or religious ecstasy, especially a supernatural appearance that usually conveys a revelation. Visions, generally, have more clarity than dreams. Most of us have a vision of how we want our story to be told or our story to be shared about our lives.

In August 2019 as a 4X Bestselling, International Author and VISIONARY Author of the Book Empowered to Win, $2^{nd}$ Edition Anthology, my vision was then manifested and I started my publishing company, **AGD Publishing**, where it is my mission to turn writers into successful authors –one book at a time.

You are Empowered to WRITE Now! For NOW! is the time for you to share your story. Now is the time to put pen/paper together (or type) your thoughts, just as God has already given you. Just like these bold and courageous women, and these young adults are sharing their truth; it's time for you to break the cycle, break the silence and WRITE YOUR OWN TRUTH!!! Speak Your Truth Because Your Story MATTERS! So, are you finally ready to be bold, strong, write, share, and publish your truth, so that you will be a blessing to others, which will encourage others to do the same; healing will take place – in so many areas of your life?

Each day we must be able to move forward and be accountable and accept the challenge to make the change in our own lives. What is a CHALLENGE? The dictionary defines a challenge as something that you want to do but have not stepped up to the plate to do it. So, this day, I CHALLENGE you to deny your fears and be brave enough to confront them. Being encouraged means to *not be conformed to this world: but be ye transformed by the renewing of your mind, that ye may prove what is that good, and acceptable, and perfect, will of God. Romans 12:2.*

> *"And the LORD answered me, and said, Write the vision, and make it plain upon tables, that he may run that readeth it." Habakkuk 2:2*

As a Life Book Writing Coach and Publisher, I encourage women and teens to think about and manage how they view their experiences dealing with situations and circumstances in their lives; it's time to stop living like victims. Here are a few things that you must do.

1. You must empower yourself through reading your daily affirmations.
2. You must know that you are of value to God.
3. You must stop looking back at your past.
4. You must stop letting small things change your destiny.

## Questions to Ponder

Identify and write down two of your weaknesses and how you can improve on these weaknesses.

1. _____

2. _____

Identify and write down two of your strengths and meditate on these strengths.

1. _____

2. _____

# HOW TO BEGIN TO WRITE YOUR STORY, YOUR CHAPTER, OR YOUR BOOK

## WHAT TO DO FIRST

- Create (draft up) an outline
- Decide on the title of your book or chapter
- Do your research
- Organize your chapters
- Keep a journal
- Manage your time
- Manage your social media accounts
- Build your email list
- Brand yourself

## WRITE DOWN YOUR THOUGHTS HERE

# Biblical Sources

Unless otherwise indicated, Scripture quotations are from the Holy Bible, King James Version (KJV). All rights reserved.

Scriptures noted: MSG (The Message) Copyright 1993, 1994, 1995, 1996, 2000, 2001, 2002. Used by permission of NavPress Publishing Group.

Scriptures noted: NIV (New International Version) Copyright 1973, 1978, 1984, 2011 by Biblica, Inc. All rights reserved.

Scriptures noted: NKJV (New King James Version) Copyright 1982 by Thomas Nelson. All rights reserved.

Scriptures noted: NLT (New Living Translation) Copyright 1996, 2004, 2007, 2013 by Tyndale House Foundation. All rights reserved.

# Are You Ready (Finally) to Write Your Story?

Now, is the time for you to share your story. Now is the time to put pen/paper together (or type) your thoughts, just as God has already given you. Just like these bold and courageous women, and these young adults are sharing their truth; it's time for you to break the cycle, break the silence and WRITE YOUR OWN TRUTH!!!

Speak Your Truth Because Your Story MATTERS!

Are you finally ready to be bold, strong, write, share, and publish your truth, so that you will be a blessing to others, which will encourage others to do the same; healing will take place -in so many areas of your life?

If you believe that this is your time, and you are ready to share your story, and you want more information about how you can be an author or a co-author email allisongdaniels@verizon.net OR visit allisongdaniels.com.

Allison G. Daniels
Visionary, Empowered to Win!

# Books Published by AGD Publishing

## CEO/FOUNDER
## ALLISON G. DANIELS

Empowered to Win, $2^{nd}$ Edition Anthology
*Allison G. Daniels, Visionary, 2021*

Spiritual Mindset
*Pastor Daniel T. Mangrum, 2020*

Exposing Shame
*Co-Pastor Sabrina A. Mangrum, 2020*

Pressing Forward
*Bishop Mary E. Adams, 2020*

Breakthrough: Book of Poems and Prayers
*Felicia Edmond, 2020*

# Published Books by Allison G. Daniels

*Untold Feelings of a Poet* (1993–2012)

*Private Fears That No One Else Hears* (1995–2012)

*Beyond Hope* (1996–2012)

*Yearning for Love* (1996–2006)

*Jesus A Joy to Call My Own* (1996–2006)

*Black Man I Love You* (1997–2005)

*Revitalizing Your Spirit* (1998–2005)

*A Glimpse of Glory* (1998–2005)

*Sweet Memories of Yesterday* (1996–2006)

*I Dream in Colors* (1998–2005)

*Facing Tomorrow* (2000)

*Taking Back My Life* (2002–2005)

ALLISON DANIELS

*Comfort Corner (2003–2006)*

*Changing Winds (2003–2006)*

*Love Expressed through A Poet (2003–2005)*

*Mother I Love You (2003)*

*Poems for all Occasions (2004–2007)*

# Books Authored by Allison G. Daniels

A Tribute to President Obama (2010–2011)

A Tribute to Whitney Houston (2012)

The Spirit of a Woman (2011–2012)

Life Goes On (2013)

Happy Valentine Day with Love (2012)

Daily Words of Wisdom (2012)

How to Self-Publish a Book (2014)

Pink Side of Me (2014)

Quotes of Wisdom (2012)

Poems for all Occasions II (2012)

When I Did When My Loved

Passed Away (2013)

ALLISON DANIELS

*Love Poems (2014)*

*Tribute to President, Barak Obama (2014)*

*Walk in Your Authority *Unleash the Divine*

*Power from Within (2016)*

# Co-Authored by Allison G. Daniels

*How to Survive When Your Ship is Sinking (2012)*

*Releasing Strongholds (2012)*

*Teenage Girls (2014)*

*The Female Leader (2012)*

*Celebration of Life (2012)*

*Bully Me No More (2013)*

*Coaching Guru Nook II (2015)*

*Sharing Our Prayers (2018)*

*Writing is Essential (2019)*

# Book Coach/Consultant

## ALLISON G. DANIELS

*Broken Peace* by Kristian Gregory-Lee

*I Believe I Can Fly* by Jackie Petty

*Behind the Chair* by Alice (Doll)

www.ingramcontent.com/pod-product-compliance
Lightning Source LLC
Chambersburg PA
CBHW030906080526
44589CB00010B/169